The Ministry Of The Holy Spirit

HARVESTIME INTERNATIONAL INSTITUTE

This course is part of the **Harvestime International Institute**, a program designed to equip believers for effective spiritual harvest.

The basic theme of the training is to teach what Jesus taught, that which took men who were fishermen, tax collectors, etc., and changed them into reproductive Christians who reached their world with the Gospel in a demonstration of power.

This manual is a single course in one of several modules of curriculum which moves believers from visualizing through deputizing, multiplying, organizing, and mobilizing to achieve the goal of evangelizing.

TABLE OF CONTENTS

HOW TO USE THIS MANUAL

MANUAL FORMAT

Each lesson consists of:

Objectives: These are the goals you should achieve by studying the chapter. Read them before starting the lesson.

Key Verse: This verse emphasizes the main concept of the chapter. Memorize it.

Chapter Content: Study each section. Use your Bible to look up any references not printed in the manual.

Self-Test: Take this test after you finish studying the chapter. Try to answer the questions without using your Bible or this manual. When you have concluded the Self-Test, check your answers in the answer section provided at the end of the book.

For Further Study: This section will help you continue your study of the Word of God, improve your study skills, and apply what you have learned to your life and ministry.

Final Examination: If you are enrolled in this course for credit, you received a final examination along with this course. Upon conclusion of this course, you should complete this examination and return it for grading as instructed.

ADDITIONAL MATERIALS NEEDED

You will need a King James version of the Bible.

SUGGESTIONS FOR GROUP STUDY

FIRST MEETING

Opening: Open with prayer and introductions. Get acquainted and register the students.

Establish Group Procedures: Determine who will lead the meetings, the time, place, and dates for the sessions.

Praise And Worship: Invite the presence of the Holy Spirit into your training session.

Distribute Manuals To Students: Introduce the manual title, format, and course objectives provided in the first few pages of the manual.

Make The First Assignment: Students will read the chapters assigned and take the Self-Tests prior to the next meeting. The number of chapters you cover per meeting will depend on chapter length, content, and the abilities of your group.

SECOND AND FOLLOWING MEETINGS

Opening: Pray. Welcome and register any new students and give them a manual. Take attendance. Have a time of praise and worship.

Review: Present a brief summary of what you studied at the last meeting.

Lesson: Discuss each section of the chapter using the **HEADINGS IN CAPITAL BOLD FACED LETTERS** as a teaching outline. Ask students for questions or comments on what they have studied. Apply the lesson to the lives and ministries of your students.

Self-Test: Review the Self-Tests students have completed. (Note: If you do not want the students to have access to the answers to the Self-Tests, you may remove the answer pages from the back of each manual.)

For Further Study: You may do these projects on a group or individual basis.

Final Examination: If your group is enrolled in this course for credit, you received a final examination with this course. Reproduce a copy for each student and administer the exam upon conclusion of this course.

Module: Deputizing
Course: The Ministry Of The Holy Spirit

INTRODUCTION

During one of his missionary trips the Apostle Paul questioned a group of believers about the Holy Spirit. He asked if they had received the Holy Spirit since they believed. Their answer was, "We have not so much as heard whether there be any Holy Ghost" (Acts 19:2).* Paul shared the message of the ministry of the Holy Spirit with these Christians (Acts 19). Today it is equally important that believers understand the ministry of the Holy Spirit. God promised:

> **And it shall come to pass in the last days, saith God, I will pour out of My Spirit upon all flesh... (Acts 2:17)**

The fact that God is willing at this time to pour out His Spirit upon us makes this study important. We must understand the ministry of the Holy Spirit in order to be part of this special revelation of the power of God. The study of the Holy Spirit is one of the major doctrines of the Bible. A doctrine is all the teachings which relate to a particular subject. Paul said:

> **...give attendance to reading, to exhortation, to doctrine. (I Timothy 4:13)**

It is not through the natural powers of man that God moves in our world. It is through the ministry of the Holy Spirit:

> **Not by might, nor by power, but by my Spirit saith the Lord. (Zechariah 4:6)**

This course examines the nature and personality of the Holy Spirit. It discusses the titles given the Holy Spirit and emblems which represent Him. Both reveal much about His ministry. The purposes, gifts, and fruit of the Holy Spirit are examined in detail. Practical guidelines are given for experiencing the baptism of the Holy Spirit, identifying spiritual gifts, and developing the fruit of the Holy Spirit.

---

* The term "Holy Ghost" used in the Bible refers to the Holy Spirit. He is called either the Holy Spirit or the Holy Ghost.

COURSE OBJECTIVES

Upon completion of this course you will be able to:

- Describe the personality of the Holy Spirit.
- List various names and titles of the Holy Spirit.
- Identify emblems representing the Holy Spirit.
- Describe the ministry of the Holy Spirit.
- Explain how to receive the baptism of the Holy Spirit.
- Receive the baptism of the Holy Spirit.
- List and define the gifts of the Spirit.
- Identify your spiritual gift(s).
- Identify the fruit of the Spirit.
- Identify the works of the flesh.
- Develop the fruit of the Holy Spirit in your life.

CHAPTER ONE

INTRODUCING THE HOLY SPIRIT

OBJECTIVES:

Upon completion of this chapter you will be able to:

- Identify the Holy Spirit as part of the Trinity of God.
- List personality traits of the Holy Spirit.
- Explain the nature of the Holy Spirit.

KEY VERSES:

> **And Jesus, when He was baptized, went up straightway out of the water; and, lo, the heavens were opened unto Him, and He saw the Spirit of God descending like a dove, and lighting upon Him;**
>
> **And lo a voice from heaven, saying, This is my beloved Son, in whom I am well pleased. (Matthew 3:16-17)**

INTRODUCTION

This chapter introduces the Holy Spirit. It explains His position in the Trinity of God, discusses His personality traits, and warns about His sensitive nature. As previously noted, the title "Holy Ghost" is used to identify the Holy Spirit. The personal pronoun "He" is also used, as the Holy Spirit is one of three persons of the Trinity of God.

Jesus spoke of the Holy Spirit as "He." Jesus said:

-He shall speak of me.	John 15:26
-I will send Him unto you.	John 16:7
-He shall glorify me.	John 16:14
-He shall not speak of Himself.	John 16:13

THE TRIUNE NATURE OF GOD

There are many gods worshiped throughout the world, but there is only one true God. The Holy Bible contains the story of this true God. The Bible is the Word of God which reveals His special plan for all mankind.

One of the things the Bible reveals is that God has a triune nature. This means His personality is revealed in three different forms. He is three persons, yet one God. The Holy Spirit is part of the triune nature of God which consists of the Father, the Son Jesus Christ, and the Holy Spirit. The three personalities are united as one in the Godhead.

Each part of the Trinity...the Father, the Son Jesus Christ, and the Holy Spirit...have special functions on behalf of mankind. This course concerns the ministry and purpose of the Holy Spirit.*

GOD, THE HOLY SPIRIT

The Holy Spirit is called God:

> **But Peter said, Ananias, why hath Satan filled thine heart to lie to the Holy Ghost...thou hast not lied unto men, but unto God. (Acts 5:3-4)**

Since He is called God, the Holy Spirit is equal with God the Father and Jesus Christ the Son. The Key Verses for this chapter reveal clearly the triune nature of God. Jesus is being baptized, the Holy Spirit descends on Him, and God speaks:

> **And Jesus, when He was baptized, went up straightway out of the water: and, lo, the heavens were opened unto Him, and He saw the Spirit of God descending like a dove, and lighting upon Him:**
>
> **And lo a voice from heaven saying, This is my beloved Son, in whom I am well pleased. (Matthew 3:16-17)**

Prior to returning to Heaven after His ministry on earth, Jesus spoke of the Holy Spirit:

> **But when the Comforter is come, whom I will send unto you from the Father, even the Spirit of truth, which proceedeth from the Father, He shall testify of me. (John 15:26)**

---

* The study of God the Father and Jesus Christ the Son is given in a separate Harvestime International Institute course entitled *"Spiritual Strategies."* An outline for study of God and Jesus is also provided in the "For Further Study" section of this chapter.

The Apostle Paul spoke of the triune nature of the Holy Spirit:

> **For the law of the Spirit of life in Christ Jesus hath made me free from the law of sin and death.**
>
> **For what the law could not do, in that it was weak through the flesh, God sending His own Son, in the likeness of sinful flesh, and for sin, condemned sin in the flesh. (Romans 8:2-3)**
>
> **The grace of the Lord Jesus Christ, and the love of God, and the communion of the Holy Ghost, be with you all. (II Corinthians 13:14)**
>
> **For through Him [the Son] we both have access by one Spirit unto the Father. (Ephesians 2:18)**

The Apostle Peter also spoke of the triune nature of God:

> **If ye be reproached for the name of Christ, happy are ye; for the Spirit of glory and of God resteth upon you: on their part He is evil spoken of, but on your part He is glorified. (I Peter 4:14)**

The book of Acts also verifies the triune nature of God:

> **Therefore being by the right hand of God exalted, and having received of the Father the promise of the Holy Ghost, He hath shed forth this, which ye now see and hear. (Acts 2:33)**

The following diagram illustrates the triune nature of God. There are three personalities...God the Father, Jesus Christ the Son, and the Holy Spirit...yet they are one God:

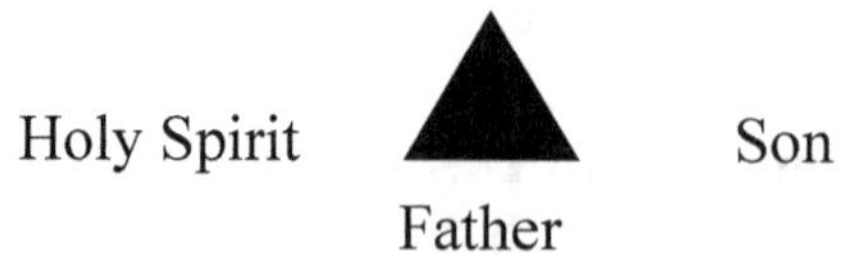

Holy Spirit ▲ Son

Father

NATURE OF THE HOLY SPIRIT

As part of the Trinity of God, the Holy Spirit has a special nature. When we speak of His nature we mean the basic qualities which describe Him. The Bible teaches that the Holy Spirit is:

OMNIPRESENT:

This means He is present everywhere:

> **Whither shall I go from thy Spirit? or whither shall I flee from thy presence? (Psalms 139:7)**

OMNISCIENT:

This means He knows all things:

> **But God hath revealed them unto us by His Spirit; for the Spirit searcheth all things, yea the deep things of God.**
>
> **For what man knoweth the things of a man, save the spirit of man which is in him? even so the things of God knoweth no man, but the Spirit of God. (I Corinthians 2:10-11)**

OMNIPOTENT:

This means the Holy Spirit is all powerful:

> **God hath spoken once; twice have I heard this; that power belongeth unto God. (Psalms 62:11)**
>
> **But ye shall receive power after that the Holy Ghost is come upon you... (Acts 1:8)**

ETERNAL:

This means He is everlasting. He had no beginning and will have no ending:

> **How much more shall the blood of Christ, who through the eternal Spirit offered Himself without spot to God, purge your conscience from dead works to serve the living God? (Hebrews 9:14)**

The eternal nature of the Holy Spirit can be illustrated by a circle. The circle has no starting or ending points, yet it exists:

The Eternal Nature Of The Holy Spirit

THE PERSONALITY OF THE HOLY SPIRIT

The Holy Spirit is part of the triune nature of God, but the Holy Spirit also has an individual personality. The Bible reveals that the Holy Spirit...

HAS A MIND:

> **And He that searcheth the hearts knoweth what is the mind of the Spirit... (Romans 8:27)**

SEARCHES OUT THE HUMAN MIND:

> **But God hath revealed them unto us by His Spirit; for the Spirit searcheth all things, yea, the deep things of God. (I Corinthians 2:10)**

HAS A WILL:

> **But all these worketh that one and the selfsame Spirit, dividing to every man severally as He will. (I Corinthians 12:11)**

The will of the Holy Spirit guides believers by denying permission for certain actions:

> **Now when they had gone throughout Phrygia and the region of Galatia, and were forbidden of the Holy Ghost to preach the word in Asia,**
>
> **After they were come to Mysia, they assayed to go into Bithynia; but the Spirit suffered them not. (Acts 16:6-7)**

The will of the Holy Spirit also guides believers by granting permission:

And after he had seen the vision, immediately we endeavored to go into Macedonia, assuredly gathering that the Lord had called us for to preach the Gospel unto them. (Acts 16:10)

SPEAKS:

He spoke to Philip:

Then the Spirit said unto Philip, Go near, and join thyself to this chariot. (Acts 8:29)

He spoke to Peter:

While Peter thought on the vision, the Spirit said unto him, Behold, three men seek thee. (Acts 10:19)

He spoke to the elders in the city of Antioch:

As they ministered to the Lord, and fasted, the Holy Ghost said, Separate me Barnabas and Saul for the work whereunto I have called them. (Acts 13:2)

Revelation chapters 2 and 3 records several messages spoken by the Holy Spirit to seven churches in Asia.

LOVES:

Now I beseech you, brethren, for the Lord Jesus Christ's sake, and for the love of the Spirit, that ye strive together with me in your prayers to God for me. (Romans 15:30)

INTERCEDES:

One of the personality traits of the Holy Spirit is that He is an intercessor. This means He prays to God on behalf of others:

Likewise the Spirit also helpeth our infirmities; for we know not what we should pray for as we ought; but the Spirit itself maketh intercession for us with groanings which cannot be uttered [spoken]. (Romans 8:26)

SENSITIVITY OF THE HOLY SPIRIT

The Holy Spirit has a sensitive nature. This means He has feelings that can be affected by the actions of man. Because of the sensitive nature of the Holy Spirit, the Bible warns that you should not:

LIE TO THE HOLY SPIRIT:

> **But Peter said, Ananias, why hath Satan filled thine heart to lie to the Holy Ghost, and to keep back part of the price of the land?**
>
> **...Thou has not lied unto me, but unto God. (Acts 5:3-4)**

RESIST THE SPIRIT:

The Holy Spirit has specific ministries on behalf of the believer which will be discussed in Chapter Three of this course. Resisting the Holy Spirit is not yielding to Him when He tries to minister in your life:

> **Ye stiffnecked and uncircumcised in heart and ears, ye do always resist the Holy Ghost: as your fathers did, so do ye. (Acts 7:51)**

QUENCH THE SPIRIT:

You quench the Holy Spirit when you refuse to do what the Holy Spirit would have you to do. The word "quench" is used elsewhere in the Bible in reference to putting out a fire. When you quench the Holy Spirit it stops the flow of His power within you. It is like throwing water on a fire. The Bible warns:

> **Quench not the Spirit. (I Thessalonians 5:19)**

GRIEVE THE SPIRIT:

Quenching the Holy Spirit is not doing what the Holy Spirit would have us do. Grieving the Holy Spirit is doing something that the Holy Spirit does NOT want us to do. The nation of Israel grieved the Holy Spirit:

> **How oft did they provoke Him in the wilderness, and grieve Him in the desert! (Psalms 78:40)**

The Bible warns:

And grieve not the Holy Spirit of God, whereby ye are sealed unto the day of redemption. (Ephesians 4:30)

INSULT THE SPIRIT:

You insult the Holy Spirit by going back into sin after you have experienced forgiveness through the blood of Jesus Christ:

Of how much sorer punishment, suppose ye, shall he be thought worthy, who hath trodden under foot the Son of God, and hath counted the blood of the covenant, wherewith he was sanctified, an unholy thing, and hath done despite unto the Spirit of grace? (Hebrews 10:29)

For it is impossible for those who were once enlightened, and have tasted of the heavenly gift, and were made partakers of the Holy Ghost,

And have tasted the good word of God, and the powers of the world to come.

If they shall fall away, to renew them again unto repentance; seeing they crucify to themselves the Son of God afresh, and put Him to an open shame. (Hebrews 6:4-6)

BLASPHEME THE SPIRIT:

Wherefore I say unto you, All manner of sin and blasphemy shall be forgiven unto men: but the blasphemy against the Holy Ghost shall not be forgiven unto men.

And whosoever speaketh a word against the Son of man, it shall be forgiven him; but whosoever speaketh against the Holy Ghost, it shall not be forgiven him, neither in this world neither in the world to come. (Matthew 12:31-32)

The sin of blasphemy against the Holy Spirit has been called the "unpardonable sin" because according to this passage it is the one sin for which there is no forgiveness. To blaspheme means to speak abusive words which reject the power of the Holy Spirit as being of God and claim it is of Satan. If a person totally rejects the power of the Holy Spirit then he can never be saved because it is the Holy Spirit which draws sinful men to Jesus Christ.

The Holy Spirit produces many visible confirming signs of God's power. Jesus was saying that if a person could not accept these miraculous signs as proof of the truth of the Gospel, then what could ever possibly convince them to believe?

VEX THE HOLY SPIRIT:

To vex the Holy Spirit means to irritate, annoy, provoke, or make angry. The Holy Spirit is vexed by the disobedience and unbelief of mankind. The Prophet Isaiah records what happened to God's people, Israel, when they vexed the Holy Spirit:

> **But they rebelled, and vexed His Holy Spirit: therefore He was turned to be their enemy, and He fought against them. (Isaiah 63:10)**

SELF-TEST

1. Write the Key Verses from memory.

____

____

2. The Holy Spirit is part of the triune nature of God which consists of God the___________, God the ________, and God the __________ __________.

3. List the six personality traits of the Holy Spirit discussed in this chapter:

__________ __________ __________ __________ __________ __________

4. What does it mean when we say the Holy Spirit has "a sensitive nature"?

____

5. Because the Holy Spirit has a sensitive nature, the Bible warns that you should not:

_______to the Holy Spirit   _________the Spirit.   __________the Spirit.

_______the Spirit.   __________the Spirit.   __________the Spirit.

_______the Spirit.

6. Read the words in list one and the definitions in list two. Write the number of the definition in front of the word which it best describes. The first is done as an example.

The Triune Nature Of The Holy Spirit

List One	**List Two**
__5__Equal	1. This means He is all powerful.
_____Omnipresent	2. This means He knows all things.
_____Omniscient	3. This means He is present everywhere.
_____Omnipotent	4. This means He is everlasting.
_____Eternal	5. This means He is one with the Father and the Son.

(Answers to tests are provided at the conclusion of the final chapter in this manual.)

FOR FURTHER STUDY

The subject of this course is the Holy Spirit who is one personality of the Trinity of God. The following outline will assist you in study of the other two persons of the Trinity, God the Father and the Son Jesus Christ.

THE TRINITY

God is a triune being composed of the Father, Son and Holy Spirit:

-The Father testified of the Son:	Matthew 3:17
-The Son testified of the Father:	John 5:19-20
-The Son testified of the Spirit:	John 14:26

GOD THE FATHER

God is Creator of all things: Nehemiah 9:6

NAMES OF GOD:

The word "God" [one who is worshiped] is a title men use to describe the Supreme Being. The Bible gives several other names for God. In the Bible names are more than an identification. They are descriptive of the bearer of the name. The names for God include:

Jehovah:	Means Lord. The Bible combines this with other names for God:
Jehovah-Rapha:	"The Lord that healeth": Exodus 15:26
Jehovah-Nissi:	"The Lord our banner": Exodus 17:8-15
Jehovah-Shalom:	"The Lord our peace": Judges 6:24
Jehovah-Ra'ah:	"The Lord my shepherd": Psalms 23:1
Jehovah-Tsidkenu:	"The Lord our righteousness": Jeremiah 23:6
Jehovah-Jireh:	"The Lord who provides": Genesis 22:14
Jehovah-Shammah:	"The Lord is there": Ezekiel 48:35
Elohim:	Which means God; used where the creative power of God is implied:
Father:	Acts 17:28; John 1:12-13
Adonai:	Means Lord or Master: Exodus 23:17; Isaiah 10:16,33
El:	This is often used in combination with other words for God:
El Shaddai:	"The God who is sufficient for the needs of His people": Exodus 6:3
Elolam:	"The everlasting God": Genesis 21:33
El Elyon:	"Most high God, exalted above all other gods": Genesis 14:18-20

In the Hebrew language in which the Old Testament was written, the word "Yahweh" means God. This word is combined with other words to reveal more about the character of God. God is called:

-Yahweh Jireh:	"The Lord provides":	Genesis 22:14
-Yahweh Nissi:	"The Lord is my banner":	Exodus 17:15
-Yahweh Shalom:	"The Lord is peace":	Judges 6:24
-Yahweh Sabbaoth:	"The Lord of Hosts":	I Samuel 1:3
-Yahweh Maccaddeshcem:	"The Lord thy Sanctifier":	Exodus 31:13
-Yahweh Roi:	"The Lord...my shepherd":	Psalms 23:1
-Yahweh Tsidkenu:	"The Lord our righteousness":	Jeremiah 23:6
-Yahweh Shammah:	"The Lord is there":	Ezekiel 48:35
-Yahweh Elohim Israel:	"The Lord God of Israel":	Judges 5:3
-Quadosh Israel:	"The Holy One of Israel":	Isaiah 1:4

WHERE IS GOD?

God's throne is in a place called Heaven, but He inhabits the whole universe also. God is everywhere: II Chronicles 16:9; Isaiah 66:1; Proverbs 15:3; Psalms 139:7-8

HOW BIG IS GOD?

God is bigger than the universe. There are no instruments of man that will measure Him: Isaiah 40:12,15,22

ATTRIBUTES OF GOD:

Attributes means characteristics. The attributes of God are listed below. God is:

A spirit: John 4:24

Infinite: [Not subject to human limitations]: I Kings 8:27; Exodus 15:18; Deuteronomy 33:27; Nehemiah 9:5; Psalms 90:2; Jeremiah 10:10; Revelation 4:8-10

One: This means He is a unity of the three persons in one: Exodus 20:3; Deuteronomy 4:35,39; 6:4; I Samuel 2:2; II Samuel 7:22; I Kings 8:60; II Kings 19:15; Nehemiah 9:6; Isaiah 44:6-8; I Timothy 1:17

Omnipotent: Genesis 1:1; 17:1; 18:14; Exodus 15:7; Deuteronomy 3:24; 32:39; I Chronicles 16:25; Job 40:2; Isaiah 40:12-15; Jeremiah 32:17; Ezekiel 10:5; Daniel 3:17; 4:35; Amos 4:13; 5:8; Zechariah 12:1; Matthew 19:26; Revelation 15:3; 19:6

Omnipresent: Genesis 28:15-16; Deuteronomy 4:39; Joshua 2:11; Proverbs 15:3; Isaiah 66:1; Jeremiah 23:23-24; Amos 9:2-4,6; Acts 7:48-49; Ephesians 1:23.

Omniscient: Genesis 18:18,19; II Kings 8:10,13; I Chronicles 28:9; Psalms 94:9; 139:1-16; 147:4-5; Proverbs 15:3; Isaiah 29:15-16; 40:28; Jeremiah 1:4,5; Ezekiel 11:5; Daniel 2:22,28; Amos 4:13; Luke 16:15; Acts 15:8,18; Romans 8:27,29; I Corinthians 3:20; II Timothy 2:19; Hebrews 4:13; I Peter 1:2; I John 3:20

Wise: Psalms 104:24; Proverbs 3:19; Jeremiah 10:12; Daniel 2:20-21; Romans 11:33; I Corinthians 1:24,25,30; 2:6-7; Ephesians 3:10; Colossians 2:2-3

Holy: Exodus 15:11; Leviticus 11:44-45; 20:26; Joshua 24:19; I Samuel 2:2: Psalms 5:4; 111:9; 145:17; Isaiah 6:3; 43:14-15; Jeremiah 23:9; Luke 1:49; James 1:13; I Peter 1:15-16; Revelation 4:8; 15:3-4

Faithful: Exodus 34:6; Numbers 23:19; Deuteronomy 4:31; Joshua 21:43-45; 23:14; I Samuel 15:29; Jeremiah 4:28; Isaiah 25:1; Ezekiel 12:25; Daniel 9:4; Micah 7:20; Luke 18:7-8; Romans 3:4; 15:8; I Corinthians 1:9; 10:13; II Corinthians 1:20; I Thessalonians 5:24; II Thessalonians 3:3; II Timothy 2:13; Hebrews 6:18; 10:23; I Peter 4:19; Revelation 15:3

Merciful: Titus 3:5; Lamentations 3:22; Daniel 9:9; Jeremiah 3:12; Psalms 32:5; Isaiah 49:13; 54:7

Loving: Deuteronomy 7:8; Ephesians 2:4; Zephaniah 3:17; Isaiah 49:15-16; Romans 8:39; Hosea 11:4; Jeremiah 31:3

Good: Psalms 25:8; Nahum 1:7; Psalms 145:9; Romans 2:4; Matthew 5:45; Psalms 31:19; Acts 14:17; Psalms 68:10; 85:5

GOD THE SON, JESUS CHRIST

LIFE OF CHRIST:

The story of Jesus Christ, the Son, is recorded in the books of Matthew, Mark, Luke, and John. Study these books for a complete record of the birth, life, death, and resurrection, and teachings of Jesus Christ.

TITLES GIVEN JESUS CHRIST:

The name "Jesus" means "Savior or deliverer": Matthew 1:21

The name "Christ" means "the anointed one: John 3:34

Additional titles given Jesus Christ in the Bible:

-The good shepherd:	John 10:11
-Light of the world:	John 8:12
-Bread of life:	John 6:48
-The way:	John 14:6
-The truth:	John 14:6
-The life:	John 14:6
-The King of kings and Lord of lords:	Revelation 19:16
-Son of man:	Matthew 17:22
-Son of David:	Matthew 1:1
-The last Adam:	I Corinthians 15:45
-Dayspring from on high:	Luke 1:78
-Son of God:	Matthew 16:16
-Only begotten Son:	John 3:16
-Chief corner stone:	Ephesians 2:20
-Great High Priest:	Hebrews 4:14
-The mediator:	Hebrews 12:24
-The lion of the tribe of Judah:	Revelation 5:5
-The Alpha and Omega [first and last]:	Revelation 1:8
-Righteous judge:	II Timothy 4:8
-King of the Jews:	Mark 15:26
-King of Israel:	John 1:49
-Author and Finisher of our faith:	Hebrews 12:2
-Blessed and only Potentate:	I Timothy 6:15
-Prince of life:	Acts 3:15
-Captain of Salvation:	Hebrews 2:10
-The Lord:	Acts 2:36
-The Savior:	John 4:42
-The Christ:	Mark 1:1
-The Logos or Word:	John 1:1,14
-The Lamb of God:	John 1:29

ATTRIBUTES OF JESUS CHRIST:

Because He is part of the Trinity of God, Jesus Christ has the same attributes as God. The Bible verifies some of these specifically in the following verses. Jesus is:

Omnipotent:	Matthew 28:18
Omniscient:	Matthew 16:30; John 21:17
Omnipresent:	Matthew 18:20; 28:20
Eternal:	John 1:1-2; 8:58
Unchangeable:	Hebrews 13:8

DEITY OF JESUS:

The book of John emphasizes the Deity of Jesus, the fact that He was part of the Godhead. Each chapter makes a reference to this. Read the selected verses on the following page and summarize each in the space provided:

1:49 ________________________	11:27 ________________________
2:11 ________________________	12:32 ________________________
3:16 ________________________	13:13 ________________________
4:26 ________________________	14:11 ________________________
5:25 ________________________	15:1 ________________________
6:33 ________________________	16:28 ________________________
7:29 ________________________	17:1 ________________________
8:58 ________________________	18:11 ________________________
9:37 ________________________	19:7 ________________________
10:30 ________________________	20:28 ________________________
	21:14 ________________________

CHAPTER TWO

REPRESENTING THE HOLY SPIRIT

OBJECTIVES:

Upon completion of this chapter you will be able to:

- Identify emblems of the Holy Spirit.
- Explain what each emblem represents.
- List titles of the Holy Spirit.

KEY VERSE:

> **Know ye not that ye are the temple of God, and that the Spirit of God dwelleth in you? (I Corinthians 3:16)**

INTRODUCTION

The titles and emblems representing the Holy Spirit provide knowledge of His nature and functions on behalf of the believer. Titles and emblems of the Holy Spirit are the subject of this chapter as we continue this introduction to the ministry of the Holy Spirit.

TITLES OF THE HOLY SPIRIT

A title is a descriptive phrase which explains a person's position and/or function. For example, if a person has the title of "President" of a country, it explains his position in government and his function as leader of the nation.

The titles given to the Holy Spirit in the Bible reveal much about His position and function. The Holy Spirit is called:

THE SPIRIT OF GOD:

> **Know ye not that ye are the temple of God, and that the Spirit of God dwelleth in you? (I Corinthians 3:16)**

THE SPIRIT OF CHRIST:

> **But ye are not in the flesh, but in the Spirit, if so be that the Spirit of God dwell in you. Now if any man have not the Spirit of Christ, he is none of His. (Romans 8:9)**

THE ETERNAL SPIRIT:

This means the Holy Spirit is everlasting, with no beginning and no end:

> **How much more shall the blood of Christ, who through the eternal Spirit offered Himself without spot to God, purge your conscience from dead works to serve the living God? (Hebrews 9:14)**

THE SPIRIT OF TRUTH:

The Holy Spirit is the source of truth which inspired God's Word, the Bible. He reveals this truth to mankind:

> **Howbeit when He, the Spirit of truth, is come, He will guide you into all truth: for He shall not speak of Himself; but whatsoever He shall hear, that shall He speak; and He will show you things to come. (John 16:13)**

THE SPIRIT OF GRACE:

> **Of how much sorer punishment, suppose ye, shall he be thought worthy, who hath trodden under foot the Son of God, and hath counted the blood of the covenant, wherewith he was sanctified, an unholy thing, and hath done despite unto the Spirit of grace. (Hebrews 10:29)**

THE SPIRIT OF LIFE:

> **For the law of the Spirit of life in Christ Jesus hath made me free from the law of sin and death. (Romans 8:2)**

THE SPIRIT OF GLORY:

> **If ye be reproached for the name of Christ, happy are ye: for the Spirit of glory and of God resteth upon you. (I Peter 4:14)**

THE SPIRIT OF WISDOM AND REVELATION:

The Holy Spirit gives wisdom to believers and reveals knowledge of Jesus Christ:

That the God of our Lord Jesus Christ, the Father of glory, may give unto you the Spirit of wisdom and revelation in the knowledge of Him. (Ephesians 1:17)

THE COMFORTER:

The Holy Spirit comforts believers in times of trouble, sorrow, and loneliness:

But the Comforter, which is the Holy Ghost, whom the Father will send in my name... (John 14:26)

THE SPIRIT OF PROMISE:

The Holy Spirit is the Spirit of promise because He is the Spirit that was sent to fulfill the promise of God:

And being assembled together with them, commanded them that they should not depart from Jerusalem, but wait for the promise of the Father, which saith, ye have heard of me.

For John truly baptized with water; but ye shall be baptized with the Holy Ghost not many days hence. (Acts 1:4-5)

THE SPIRIT OF HOLINESS:

And declared to be the Son of God with power, according to the Spirit of holiness, by the resurrection from the dead. (Romans 1:4)

THE SPIRIT OF FAITH:

We having the same spirit of faith, according as it is written, I believe and therefore have I spoken; we also believe, and therefore speak. (II Corinthians 4:13)

THE SPIRIT OF ADOPTION:

It is through the Holy Spirit that we are "adopted" into the family of God as the children of God:

For ye have not received the spirit of bondage again to fear; but ye have received the Spirit of adoption, whereby we cry, Abba, Father. (Romans 8:15)

EMBLEMS OF THE HOLY SPIRIT

The Bible uses several emblems to represent the Holy Spirit. An emblem represents something. It is a symbol which has a special meaning. The following are emblems used in the Bible to represent the Holy Spirit:

THE DOVE:

The Holy Spirit was revealed in the form of a dove at the time of the baptism of Jesus. This emblem of the Holy Spirit indicates approval, purity, and peace:

> **And John bare record, saying, I saw the Spirit descending from heaven like a dove, and it abode upon Him. (John 1:32)**

Approval:

> **And John bare record, saying, I saw the Spirit descending from heaven like a dove, and it abode upon Him. (John 1:32)**

Peace:

> **And I said, Oh that I had wings like a dove! for then would I fly away, and be at rest. (Psalms 55:6)**

Purity:

> **My dove, my undefiled, is but one... (Song of Solomon 6:9)**

OIL:

Oil is used in the Bible as a symbol or emblem of the Holy Spirit. Oil indicates light, healing, and anointing for service. All of these are given to a believer through the Holy Spirit.

> **The Spirit of the Lord is upon me, because He hath anointed me to preach the gospel to the poor; He hath sent me to heal the broken-hearted, to preach deliverance to the captives, and recovering of sight to the blind, to set at liberty them that are bruised. (Luke 4:18)**

> **How God anointed Jesus of Nazareth with the Holy Ghost and with power: who went about doing good, and healing all that were oppressed of the devil; for God was with Him. (Acts 10:38)**

Thou hast loved righteousness, and hated iniquity; therefore God, even thy God, hath anointed thee with the oil of gladness above thy fellows. (Hebrews 1:9)

WATER:

Water signifies the new life and cleansing from sin that the Holy Spirit brings to the believer. Jesus spoke of the Holy Spirit being like water:

In the last day, that great day of the feast, Jesus stood and cried, saying, If any man thirst let him come unto me, and drink.

He that believeth on me, as the scripture hath said, out of his belly shall flow rivers of living water.

But this spake He of the Spirit, which they that believe on Him should receive; for the Holy Ghost was not yet given; because that Jesus was not yet glorified. (John 7:37-39)

For I will pour water upon him that is thirsty, and floods upon the dry ground: I will pour my Spirit upon thy seed, and my blessing upon thine offspring. (Isaiah 44:3)

A SEAL:

A seal is a special mark indicating ownership. It also indicates a finished transaction. The Holy Spirit has sealed believers as belonging to God. It indicates their salvation is a finished work.

In whom ye also trusted, after that ye heard the word of truth, the gospel of your salvation: in whom also, after that ye believed, were sealed with that Holy Spirit of promise. (Ephesians 1:13)

And grieve not the Holy Spirit of God, whereby ye are sealed unto the day of redemption. (Ephesians 4:30)

Who hath also sealed us, and given the earnest of the Spirit in our hearts. (II Corinthians 1:22)

WIND:

The wind is also an emblem of the Holy Spirit. It represents the power of the Holy Spirit:

> **The wind bloweth where it listeth, and thou hearest the sound thereof, but canst not tell whence it cometh, and whither it goeth; so is every one that is born of the Spirit. (John 3:8)**
>
> **And when the day of Pentecost was fully come, they were all with one accord in one place.**
>
> **And suddenly there came a sound from heaven as of a rushing mighty wind, and it filled all the house where they were sitting. (Acts 2:1-2)**

You cannot see the wind in the natural world, but you can certainly see visible effects of the wind. In the natural world the wind has special functions. These functions are natural parallels of the functions of the "wind" of the Holy Spirit:

Wind Produces Life:

It scatters seeds as it blows and this brings new growth. The Holy Spirit produces life through the seeds of the Word of God as they are scattered in the hearts and minds of men. This life is not only eternal life of salvation, but mature spiritual life through spiritual fruit which result from the seed of the Word.

Wind Separates The Wheat From The Chaff:

It purifies as it blows away the debris. The Holy Spirit serves as a purifying power in the life of the believer.

Wind Fans Dying Coals And Sets Them Ablaze:

The wind of the Holy Spirit "fans" God's people in revival and makes them a flaming fire of ministry to the world.

FIRE:

Fire is another emblem of the Holy Spirit. Fire signifies:

The Presence Of The Lord:

> **And the Angel of the Lord appeared unto him in a flame of fire out of the midst of the bush: and he looked, and behold, the bush burned with fire, and the bush was not consumed. (Exodus 3:2)**

Approval Of The Lord:

> **And there came a fire out from before the Lord, and consumed upon the altar the burnt offering and the fat; and when the people saw, they shouted, and fell on their faces. (Leviticus 9:24)**

Protection And Guidance:

> **And the Lord went before them by day in a pillar of a cloud, to lead them in the way; and by night in a pillar of fire, to give them light; to go by day and night. (Exodus 13:21)**

Purifying:

Isaiah 6:1-8 tells of the Prophet Isaiah being purified by the fire of the Holy Spirit. Read this passage in your Bible.

The Gift Of The Holy Spirit:

When the Holy Spirit was first given, fire was used as a symbol of His presence:

> **And there appeared unto them cloven tongues like as of fire, and it sat upon each of them. (Acts 2:3)**

Judgment:

> **For our God is a consuming fire. (Hebrews 12:29)**

REPRESENTING THE HOLY SPIRIT

The names and emblems representing the Holy Spirit reveal only some of His purposes and ministry. Additional ministries of the Holy Spirit are detailed in the next chapter.

SELF-TEST

1. Write the Key Verse from memory.

____

2. What is an emblem?

____

3. Read the list of emblems of the Holy Spirit in list one. Read the definitions in list two. Write the number of the definition on the blank in front of the emblem which it best describes.

Emblems Of The Holy Spirit

List One	**List Two**
_____Wind	1. Stands for purity and peace.
_____A seal	2. Indicates light, healing, anointing for service.
_____Water	3. Indicates life and cleansing.
_____A dove	4. Indicates ownership.
_____Oil	5. Indicates power.

4. Fire is an emblem of the Holy Spirit. List the six things that fire signifies:

______________________________ ______________________________

______________________________ ______________________________

______________________________ ______________________________

5. Thirteen titles of the Holy Spirit were discussed in this chapter. How many can you list?

__________ __________ __________ __________ __________ __________

__________ __________ __________ __________ __________ __________

____

(Answers to tests are provided at the conclusion of the final chapter in this manual.)

FOR FURTHER STUDY

In the New Testament there are 261 passages which refer to the Holy Spirit. He is mentioned:

-56 times in the Gospels of Matthew, Mark, Luke and John.
-57 times in the book of Acts.
-148 times in the remaining New Testament.

Read the entire New Testament through. As you read, circle each mention of the Holy Spirit. Study these passages to increase your knowledge of the ministry of the Holy Spirit.

CHAPTER THREE

THE MINISTRY OF THE HOLY SPIRIT

OBJECTIVES:

Upon completion of this chapter you will be able to:

Explain the ministry of the Holy Spirit concerning:
- Creation
- Scriptures
- Israel
- Satan
- Jesus
- The sinner
- The Church
- Believers

KEY VERSE:

> **But the Comforter, which is the Holy Ghost, whom the Father will send in my name, He shall teach you all things, and bring all things to your remembrance, whatsoever I have said unto you. (John 14:26)**

INTRODUCTION

The purpose of this chapter is to describe the ministries of the Holy Spirit from creation of the world through His present ministry to believers.

CREATION

The Holy Spirit was active in creation of the earth:

> **And the earth was without form, and void; and darkness was upon the face of the deep. And the Spirit of God moved upon the face of the waters. (Genesis 1:2)**

> **Thou sendest forth thy spirit, they are created: and thou renewest the face of the earth. (Psalms 104:30)**

SCRIPTURES

The Holy Spirit's ministry involves the written Word of God which is called the Holy Scriptures or the Holy Bible. The Holy Spirit ministered by:

REVELATION:

He spoke to human writers the message of God:

> **For the prophecy came not in old time by the will of man but holy men of God spake as they were moved by the Holy Ghost. (II Peter 1:21)**

INSPIRATION:

He guided these writers so the message would be accurate:

> **All scripture is given by inspiration of God, and is profitable for doctrine, for reproof, for correction, for instruction in righteousness;**
>
> **That the man of God may be perfect, thoroughly furnished unto all good works. (II Timothy 3:16-17)**

ILLUMINATION:

He enlightens human hearts to understand the message of the Gospel:

> **But the Comforter, which is the Holy Ghost, whom the Father will send in my name, He shall teach you all things, and bring all things to your remembrance, whatsoever I have said unto you. (John 14:26)**

ISRAEL

The nation of Israel was chosen by God as a people through which He could reveal Himself and fulfill His master plan in the world. was through Israel that the Messiah came to save men from sin. The experiences of Israel provided an example both of success and failure for believers. From Jerusalem, the capital of Israel, the Gospel message spread throughout the world.

The ministry of the Holy Spirit to Israel is evident from the very beginning of the nation. The Holy Spirit:

CAME UPON THE LEADERS OF ISRAEL:

There are too many examples of this to reproduce all the verses as part of this manual. The references are listed in the "For Further Study" section of this chapter. Study of this subject will provide understanding of how the Holy Spirit moved in the lives of people during Old Testament times.

CAME UPON ISRAEL'S PLACES OF WORSHIP:

> **Then a cloud covered the tent of the congregation, and the glory of the Lord filled the tabernacle. (Exodus 40:34)**
>
> **And it came to pass, when the priests were come out of the holy place, that the cloud filled the house of the Lord. (I Kings 8:10)**

GUIDED THEM TO THE PROMISED LAND:

> **Thou gavest also thy good spirit to instruct them, and withheldest not thy manna from their mouth, and gavest them water for their thirst.**
>
> **Yea, forty years didst thou sustain them in the wilderness so that they lacked nothing... (Nehemiah 9:20)**

WILL COME UPON ISRAEL DURING THE TRIBULATION:

The tribulation is a future time of great trouble on the earth. God will place a special mark of protection on Israel.

> **And I saw another angel ascending from the east, having the seal of the living God: and he cried with a loud voice to the four angels, to whom it was given to hurt the earth and the sea,**
>
> **Saying, Hurt not the earth, neither the sea, nor the trees, till we have sealed the servants of our God in their foreheads.**
>
> **And I heard the number of them which were sealed: and there were sealed an hundred and forty and four thousand of all the tribes of the children of Israel. (Revelation 7:2-4)**

WILL COME UPON ISRAEL DURING THE MILLENNIUM:

The Millennium is a thousand years of peace during which Jesus will reign on the earth:

And I will pour upon the house of David, and upon the inhabitants of Jerusalem, the spirit of grace and supplications: and they shall look upon me whom they have pierced, and they shall mourn for Him, as one mourneth for his only son, and shall be in bitterness for Him, as one that is in bitterness for his firstborn. (Zechariah 12:10)

SATAN

The Holy Spirit even has a ministry concerning Satan. The Holy Spirit is the restraining spiritual force that limits the power of Satan:

...When the enemy shall come in like a flood, the Spirit of the Lord shall lift up a standard against him. (Isaiah 59:19)

When the Holy Spirit is removed from the world, then the spirit of the antichrist will have control for a period of time. The antichrist will be an evil world leader:

For the mystery of iniquity doeth already work: only he who now letteth will let, until he be taken out of the way.

And then shall that Wicked be revealed, whom the Lord shall consume, with the spirit of His mouth, and shall destroy with the brightness of His coming;

Even him, whose coming is after the working of Satan with all power and signs and lying wonders.

And with all deceivableness of unrighteousness in them that perish; because they received not the love of the truth, that they might be saved,

And for this cause God shall send them strong delusion that they should believe a lie;

That they all might be damned who believed not the truth but had pleasure in unrighteousness. (II Thessalonians 2:7-12)

JESUS

The ministry of the Holy Spirit was evident in the life of Jesus. Jesus was:

CONCEIVED BY THE SPIRIT:

And the angel answered and said unto her, The Holy Ghost shall come upon thee, and the power of the Highest shall overshadow thee; therefore also that

holy thing which shall be born of thee shall be called the Son of God. (Luke 1:35)

Now the birth of Jesus Christ was on this wise, when as his mother Mary was espoused to Joseph, before they came together, she was found with child of the Holy Ghost...

Behold, the angel of the Lord appeared unto him in a dream, saying, Joseph, thou son of David, fear not to take unto thee Mary thy wife: for that which is conceived in her is of the Holy Ghost. (Matthew 1:18,20)

ANOINTED BY THE SPIRIT:

And Jesus, when He was baptized, went up straightway out of the water: and, lo, the heavens were opened unto Him, and He saw the Spirit of God descending like a dove, and lighting upon Him... (Matthew 3:16)

The Spirit of the Lord is upon me, because He hath anointed me to preach the gospel to the poor, He hath sent me to heal the brokenhearted, to preach deliverance to the captives and recovering of sight to the blind, to set at liberty them that are bruised... (Luke 4:18)

How God anointed Jesus of Nazareth with the Holy Ghost and with power: who went about doing good, and healing all that were oppressed of the devil; for God was with Him. (Acts 10:38)

Thou hast loved righteousness, and hated iniquity; therefore God, even thy God, hath anointed thee with the oil of gladness above thy fellows. (Hebrews 1:9)

SEALED BY THE SPIRIT:

Labour not for the meat which perisheth, but for that meat which endureth unto everlasting life, which the Son of man shall give unto you: for Him hath God the Father sealed. (John 6:27)

LED BY THE SPIRIT:

Then was Jesus led up of the Spirit into the wilderness to be tempted of the devil. (Matthew 4:1)

EMPOWERED BY THE SPIRIT:

But if I cast out devils by the Spirit of God, then the kingdom of God is come unto you. (Matthew 12:28)

FILLED BY THE SPIRIT:

And Jesus, being full of the Holy Ghost returned from Jordan, and was led by the Spirit into the wilderness. (Luke 4:1)

For He whom God hath sent speaketh the words of God; for God giveth not the Spirit by measure unto Him. (John 3:34)

TROUBLED IN THE SPIRIT:

When Jesus therefore saw her weeping, and the Jews also weeping which came with her, He groaned in the spirit and was troubled. (John 11:33)

REJOICED IN THE SPIRIT:

In that hour Jesus rejoiced in spirit and said, I thank thee, O Father, Lord of heaven and earth, that thou hast hid these things from the wise and prudent, and hast revealed them unto babes: even so, Father; for so it seemed good in thy sight. (Luke 10:21)

OFFERED THROUGH THE SPIRIT:

How much more shall the blood of Christ, who through the eternal Spirit offered Himself without spot to God, purge your conscience from dead works to serve the living God? (Hebrews 9:14)

RAISED BY THE SPIRIT:

For Christ also hath once suffered for sins, the just for the unjust, that He might bring us to God, being put to death in the flesh, but quickened by the Spirit. (I Peter 3:18)

And declared to be the Son of God with power, according to the Spirit of holiness, by the resurrection from the dead. (Romans 1:4)

COMMANDED HIS DISCIPLES THROUGH THE SPIRIT:

Until the day in which He was taken up, after that He through the Holy

Ghost had given commandments unto the apostles whom he had chosen. (Acts 1:2)

SINNERS

The Holy Spirit's ministry concerning the sinner was described by Jesus:

> **Nevertheless I tell you the truth; It is expedient for you that I go away; for if I go not away, the Comforter will not come unto you; but if I depart, I will send Him unto you.**
>
> **And when He is come, He will reprove the world of sin, and of righteousness, and of judgment:**
>
> **Of sin, because they believe not on me;**
>
> **Of righteousness because I go to my Father and ye see me no more;**
>
> **Of judgment because the prince of this world is judged. (John 16:7-11)**

THE CHURCH

The Holy Spirit serves several purposes in the Church. He...

FORMED IT:

> Now therefore ye are no more strangers and foreigners, but fellow citizens with the saints, and of the household of God;
>
> And are built upon the foundation of the apostles and prophets, Jesus Christ Himself being the chief corner stone;
>
> In whom all the building fitly framed together groweth unto a holy temple in the Lord;
>
> In whom ye also are builded together for a habitation of God through the Spirit. (Ephesians 2:19-22)

INSPIRES ITS WORSHIP:

> **For we are the circumcision, which worship God in the Spirit, and rejoice in Christ Jesus, and have no confidence in the flesh. (Philippians 3:3)**

DIRECTS ITS MISSIONARY ACTIVITIES:

Then the Spirit said unto Philip, Go near, and join thyself to this chariot. (Acts 8:29)

Now when they had gone throughout Phrygia and the region of Galatia, and were forbidden of the Holy Ghost to preach the word in Asia,

After they were come to Mysia, they assayed to go into Bithynia; but the Spirit suffered them not.

And after he had seen the vision, immediately we endeavored to go into Macedonia, assuredly gathering that the Lord had called us for to preach the gospel unto them. (Acts 16:6,7,10)

As they ministered to the Lord, and fasted, the Holy Ghost said, Separate me Barnabas and Saul for the work whereunto I have called them.

So they, being sent forth by the Holy Ghost, departed unto Seleucia; and from thence they sailed to Cyprus. (Acts 13:2,4)

SELECTS ITS MINISTERS:

Take heed therefore unto yourselves, and to all the flock, over the which the Holy Ghost hath made you overseers, to feed the church of God, which He hath purchased with His own blood. (Acts 20:28)

ANOINTS ITS PREACHERS:

And my speech and my preaching was not with enticing words of man's wisdom, but in demonstration of the Spirit and of power. (I Corinthians 2:4)

GUIDES ITS DECISIONS:

For it seemed good to the Holy Ghost and to us, to lay upon you no greater burden than these necessary things. (Acts 15:28)

BAPTIZES IT WITH POWER:

And when the day of Pentecost was fully come, they were all with one accord in one place.

And suddenly there came a sound from heaven as of a rushing mighty wind, and it filled all the house where they were sitting.

And there appeared unto them cloven tongues like as a fire, and it sat upon each of them.

And they were all filled with the Holy Ghost and began to speak with other tongues, as the Spirit gave them utterance. (Acts 2:1-4)

BELIEVERS

The Holy Spirit serves an important purpose in the lives of believers. He...

CONVICTS:

It is the Holy Spirit that convicts of sin to draw men and women to Jesus. You could not become a believer without this ministry of the Spirit:

And when He is come, He will reprove the world of sin, and of righteousness, and of judgment:

Of sin, because they believe not on me;

Of righteousness, because I go to My Father and ye see me no more;

Of judgment, because the prince of this world is judged. (John 16:8-11)

REGENERATES:

The Holy Spirit changes your life when you become a believer:

Not by works of righteousness which we have done, but according to His mercy He saved us, by the washing of regeneration, and renewing of the Holy Ghost. (Titus 3:5)

Jesus answered and said unto him, Verily, verily, I say unto thee, Except a man be born again, he cannot see the kingdom of God.

Nicodemus saith unto Him, How can a man be born when he is old? can he enter the second time into his mother's womb, and be born?

Jesus answered, Verily, verily, I say unto thee, Except a man be born of water and of the Spirit, he cannot enter into the kingdom of God.

That which is born of the flesh is flesh; and that which is born of the Spirit is spirit.

Marvel not that I said unto thee, Ye must be born again. (John 3:3-7)

SANCTIFIES:

The Holy Spirit takes this life which has been changed by salvation and enables righteous living:

But we are bound to give thanks alway to God for you, brethren, beloved of the Lord, because God hath from the beginning chosen you to salvation through sanctification of the Spirit and belief of the truth...
(II Thessalonians 2:13)

BAPTIZES:

Chapter Four of this manual deals with this experience of baptism in the Holy Spirit:

And they were all filled with the Holy Ghost and began to speak in other tongues, as the Spirit gave them utterance. (Acts 2:4)

DWELLS WITHIN:

The purpose of this indwelling is to strengthen the new nature received through salvation:

What! Know ye not that your body is the temple of the Holy Ghost which is in you, which ye have of God, and ye are not your own?
(I Corinthians 6:19)

Know ye not that ye are the temple of God, and that the Spirit of God dwelleth in you? (I Corinthians 3:16)

Therefore if any man be in Christ, he is a new creature; old things are passed away; behold all things are become new. (II Corinthians 5:17)

This I say then, Walk in the Spirit, and ye shall not fulfill the lust of the flesh.

For the flesh lusteth against the Spirit, and the Spirit against the flesh; and these are contrary the one to the other; so that ye cannot do the things that ye would.

But if ye be led of the Spirit, ye are not under the law. (Galatians 5:16-18)

In the natural world, after a house has been lived in by a person for a period of time it reflects the character of that person. Likewise, our spiritual houses should reflect the character of the Holy Spirit who dwells within.

STRENGTHENS:

That He would grant you, according to the riches of His glory, to be strengthened with might by His Spirit in the inner man. (Ephesians 3:16)

UNITES:

The Holy Spirit makes a believer one in spirit with God and other believers. This is called the "unity of the Spirit":

But he that is joined unto the Lord is one spirit. (I Corinthians 6:17)

For as the body is one, and hath many members, and all the members of that one body, being many are one body: so also is Christ.

For by one Spirit are we all baptized into one body, whether we be Jews or Gentiles, whether we be bond or free; and have been all made to drink into one Spirit. (I Corinthians 12:12-13)

INTERCEDES:

Likewise the Spirit also helpeth our infirmities: for we know not what we should pray for as we ought: but the Spirit itself maketh intercession for us with groanings which cannot be uttered. (Romans 8:26)

But ye, beloved, building up yourselves on your most holy faith, praying in the Holy Ghost. (Jude 20)

Praying always with all prayer and supplication in the Spirit, and watching thereunto with all perseverance and supplication for all saints. (Ephesians 6:18)

GUIDES:

Howbeit when He, the Spirit of truth, is come, He will guide you into all truth; for He shall not speak of Himself; but whatsoever He shall hear, that shall He speak; and He will show you things to come. (John 16:13)

For as many as are led by the Spirit of God, they are the sons of God. (Romans 8:14)

DEMONSTRATES LOVE:

The Holy Spirit shows the love of Christ to and through the believer:

And hope maketh not ashamed; because the love of God is shed abroad in our hearts by the Holy Ghost which is given unto us. (Romans 5:5)

CONFORMS TO THE IMAGE OF CHRIST:

The Holy Spirit conforms the believer to the image of Christ:

But we all, with open face beholding as in a glass the glory of the Lord, are changed into the same image from glory to glory, even as by the Spirit of the Lord. (II Corinthians 3:18)

REVEALS TRUTH:

But God hath revealed them unto us by His Spirit: for the Spirit searcheth all things, yea, the deep things of God. (I Corinthians 2:10)

TEACHES:

But the anointing which ye have received of Him abideth in you, and ye need not that any man teach you: but as the same anointing teacheth you of all things, and is truth, and is no lie, and even as it hath taught you, ye shall abide in Him. (I John 2:27)

ASSURES OF SALVATION:

The Spirit itself beareth witness, with our spirit, that we are the children of God. (Romans 8:16)

And he that keepeth His commandments dwelleth in Him, and He in him. And hereby we know that He abideth in us, by the Spirit which He hath given us. (I John 3:24)

GIVES LIBERTY:

For the law of the Spirit of life in Christ Jesus hath made me free from the law of sin and death. (Romans 8:2)

Now the Lord is that Spirit: and where the Spirit of the Lord is, there is liberty. (II Corinthians 3:17)

COMFORTS:

...and walking in the fear of the Lord, and in the comfort of the Holy Ghost... (Acts 9:31)

Even the Spirit of truth, whom the world cannot receive, because it seeth Him not, neither knoweth Him; but ye know Him; for He dwelleth with you, and shall be in you...

But the Comforter , which is the Holy Ghost, whom the Father will send in my name, He shall teach you all things and bring all things to your remembrance, whatsoever I have said unto you. (John 14:17,26)

QUICKENS:

But if the Spirit of Him that raised up Jesus from the dead dwell in you, He that raised up Christ from the dead shall also quicken [empower, give new life, resurrect] your mortal bodies by His Spirit that dwelleth in you. (Romans 8:11)

SPEAKS:

But when they shall lead you, and deliver you up, take no thought beforehand what ye shall speak, neither do ye premeditate; but whatsoever shall be given you in that hour, that speak ye: for it is not ye that speak, but the Holy Ghost. (Mark 13:11)

DEMONSTRATES GOD'S POWER:

And my speech and my preaching was not with enticing words of man's wisdom, but in demonstration of the Spirit and of power;

That your faith should not stand in the wisdom of men but in the power of God. (I Corinthians 2:4-5)

INSPIRES WORSHIP:

God is a Spirit: and they that worship Him must worship Him in spirit and in truth. (John 4:24)

EMPOWERS FOR WITNESSING:

The power to witness is the true evidence that one has been baptized in the Holy Spirit.

> **But ye shall receive power, after that the Holy Ghost is come upon you; and ye shall be witnesses unto me both in Jerusalem, and in all Judaea, and in Samaria, and unto the uttermost parts of the earth. (Acts 1:8)**

GIVES GIFTS AND DEVELOPS FRUIT:

The Holy Spirit gives spiritual gifts to believers. These are specific abilities to enable him to function effectively as part of the Church. The Holy Spirit also develops spiritual fruit in a believer's life. Spiritual fruit refers to the nature of the Holy Spirit in the life of a believer. Because of their importance, the fruit and gifts of the Holy Spirit are discussed in separate chapters.

SELF-TEST

1. Write the Key Verse from memory.

____

____

2. List five purposes of the Holy Spirit in relation to the nation of Israel.

__________ __________ __________ __________ __________

3. Is this statement true or false? The Holy Spirit was involved in creation of the earth.

   The statement is:_____________________

4. Write the number of the correct meaning in front of the word which it describes.

Purposes Of The Holy Spirit
In Relation In Scripture

_____Illumination	1. He spoke to human writers the message of God.
_____Revelation	2. The present ministry of the Holy Spirit which helps people understand the Gospel.
_____Inspiration	3. The Spirit guided the writers so the message would be accurate.

5. Give a Scripture reference which explains the purpose of the Holy Spirit in the life of a sinner.

____

6. What is the ministry of the Holy Spirit in regard to Satan?

____

7. This chapter listed eleven purposes of the Holy Spirit in the life of Jesus Christ. How many of these can you list?

___________ ___________ ___________ ___________ ___________

___________ ___________ ___________ ___________ ___________

____

8. This chapter discussed seven purposes of the Holy Spirit in the Church. How many can you list?

___________ ___________ ___________ ___________ ___________

___________ ___________

9. This chapter discussed twenty purposes of the Holy Spirit in the life of a believer. How many can you list?

___________ ___________ ___________ ___________ ___________

___________ ___________ ___________ ___________ ___________

___________ ___________ ___________ ___________ ___________

___________ ___________ ___________ ___________ ___________

10. What is the true evidence that a person has been baptized in the Holy Spirit?

____

(Answers to tests are provided at the conclusion of the final chapter in this manual.)

FOR FURTHER STUDY

1. Study the following Bible passages to learn more about the ministry of the Holy Spirit to the nation of Israel:

   Genesis 41:38
   Numbers 11:17; 11:25; 27:18
   Judges 3:10; 6:34; 11:29; 14:6,19; 15:14-15
   I Samuel 10:10; 11:6; 16:13
   I Kings 18:12
   II Kings 2:15-16
   Ezekiel 2:2
   Daniel 4:9; 5:11; 6:3
   Micah 3:8
   II Chronicles 15:1; 24:20

2. Review the purposes of the Holy Spirit in the life of a believer. Are you allowing the Holy Spirit to serve in each of these areas in your life?

____

____

____

3. Review the ministries of the Holy Spirit to the Church. Think about the church fellowship you attend... In which areas are they allowing the Holy Spirit to serve His purposes? In which areas is improvement needed?

____

____

____

CHAPTER FOUR

THE BAPTISM OF THE HOLY SPIRIT

OBJECTIVES:

Upon completion of this chapter you will be able to:

- Define baptize.
- Identify three Scriptural references where it reveals what happened when people receive the baptism of the Holy Spirit.
- Explain how to receive the Baptism of the Holy Spirit.
- Identify the outward physical sign of the baptism of the Holy Spirit.
- Explain the true evidence of baptism in the Holy Spirit.
- List guidelines for receiving the baptism of the Holy Spirit.
- Receive the baptism of the Holy Spirit.
- List four main objections people sometimes raise to the baptism of the Holy Spirit.

KEY VERSE:

> **But ye shall receive power after that the Holy Ghost is come upon you: and ye shall be witnesses unto me both in Jerusalem, and in all Judaea, and in Samaria, and unto the uttermost part of the earth. (Acts 1:8)**

INTRODUCTION

The Bible speaks of four different baptisms:

1. The baptism of suffering experienced by Jesus.
2. The water baptism performed by John the Baptist.
3. Christian baptism in water.
4. Baptism of the Holy Spirit.

This chapter concerns the baptism of the Holy Spirit. (The other three baptisms are discussed in the Harvestime International Institute course entitled *"Foundations Of Faith"*).

DEFINITION

The word "baptize" means to completely immerse or submerge in something.

PROMISE OF THE BAPTISM

After the resurrection and prior to His return to Heaven, Jesus gave important instructions to His followers:

> **And behold, I send the promise of my Father upon you: but tarry ye in the city of Jerusalem until ye be endued with power from on high. (Luke 24:49)**

The promise to which Jesus referred was the Holy Spirit:

> **And I will pray the Father and He shall give you another Comforter, that He may abide with you for ever;**
>
> **Even the Spirit of truth; whom the world cannot receive, because it seeth Him not, neither knoweth Him; but ye know Him; for He dwelleth with you and shall be in you.**
>
> **I will not leave you comfortless. (John 14:16-18)**

This was not a new promise. The gift of the Holy Spirit had been promised since Old Testament times:

> **...for with stammering lips and another tongue will He speak to this people.**
>
> **To whom He said, This is the rest wherewith ye may cause the weary to rest, and this is the refreshing...(Isaiah 28:11-12)**
>
> **...I will pour out my Spirit upon all flesh...(Joel 2:28)**

THE EVIDENCE OF THE HOLY SPIRIT

As you learned in a previous chapter, the Holy Spirit has many purposes in the lives of believers. One of the main purposes of the Holy Spirit, however, is to make the Christian a powerful witness for the Gospel:

> **But ye shall receive power after that the Holy Ghost is come upon you; and ye shall be witnesses unto me...to the uttermost part of the earth. (Acts 1:8)**

The true evidence of the baptism of the Holy Spirit was visible immediately in the life of the Apostle Peter. Before the Day of Pentecost he had fearfully denied that he knew Jesus. After his baptism in the Holy Spirit, Peter stood and gave a powerful witness to the Gospel that resulted in the salvation of 3,000 people.

It was the power of the Holy Spirit in the early church that resulted in the spread of the Gospel throughout the world. The book of Acts is a record of this powerful witness which was evidence of baptism in the Holy Spirit.

BAPTISM IN THE HOLY SPIRIT

There are seven passages in the New Testament where the word "baptize" is used in relation to the Holy Spirit. Four of these are the words of John the Baptist recorded in the Gospels:

> **I indeed baptize you with water unto repentance: but he that cometh after me is mightier than I, whose shoes I am not worthy to bear: He shall baptize you with the Holy Ghost, and with fire. (Matthew 3:11)**

> **I indeed have baptized you with water: but He shall baptize you with the Holy Ghost. (Mark 1:8)**

> **John answered, saying unto them all, I indeed baptize you with water; but one mightier than I cometh, the latchet of whose shoes I am not worthy to unloose; He shall baptize you with the Holy Ghost and with fire. (Luke 3:16)**

> **And I knew Him not: but He that sent me to baptize with water, the same said unto me, Upon whom thou shalt see the Spirit descending and remaining on Him, the same is He which baptizeth with the Holy Ghost. (John 1:33)**

Jesus also spoke of the baptism of the Holy Ghost:

> **For John truly baptized with water; but ye shall be baptized with the Holy Ghost not many days hence. (Acts 1:5)**

When Peter spoke of events which took place in the home of Cornelius he quoted the words of Jesus:

> **Then remembered I the word of the Lord, how that He said, John indeed baptized with water; but ye shall be baptized with the Holy Ghost. (Acts 11:16)**

Paul also used the word "baptize" in relation to the Holy Spirit:

For by one Spirit are we all baptized into one body, whether we be Jews or Gentiles, whether we be bond or free; and have been all made to drink into one Spirit. (I Corinthians 12:13)

Use of the phrase "to baptize into" the Holy Spirit is the same as used to describe Christian baptism in water. In both cases baptism is an outward confirmation of an inward spiritual experience.

The Holy Spirit was given during a time of Jewish observance called the feast of Pentecost. For this reason, baptism in the Holy Spirit is often called a "Pentecostal experience" and the time of the giving of the Spirit called "the day of Pentecost."

The Holy Spirit came down from Heaven and completely immersed [baptized] believers assembled in the upper room of a house in Jerusalem. They had been waiting or "tarrying" for His coming as they had been commanded to do by Jesus. Peter said this experience was the fulfillment of God's promise,"In the last days...I will pour out of my Spirit upon all flesh." This promise was given by the prophet Joel:

And it shall come to pass afterward, that I will pour out my Spirit upon all flesh; and your sons and your daughters shall prophesy, your old men shall dream dreams, your young men shall see visions;

And also upon the servants and upon the handmaids in those days will I pour out my spirit. (Joel 2:28-29)

Male and female, young and old were to be included in this outpouring of the Holy Spirit. They were to prophesy, dream dreams, and see visions. God's Spirit was to empower both servants [men] and handmaidens [women]. On the day the Holy Spirit was given, Peter said:

Repent and be baptized every one of you in the name of Jesus Christ for the remission of sins, and ye shall receive the gift of the Holy Ghost.

For the promise is unto you, and to your children, and to all that are afar off, even as many as the Lord our God shall call. (Acts 2:38-39)

Peter's words revealed that the promise of the Holy Spirit was:

-A national promise: "Unto you" [the Jewish people].
-A family promise: "Your children."
-A universal promise: "To all that are afar off."

THE PHYSICAL SIGN

The Holy Spirit is invisible to the natural eye. He was compared by Jesus to the wind:

> **The wind bloweth where it listeth, and thou hearest the sound thereof, but canst not tell whence it cometh, and whither it goeth: so is every one that is born of the Spirit. (John 3:8)**

Although the wind is invisible, the effects it produces can be seen and heard. When the wind blows the dust rises from the ground, the trees all bend in one direction, leaves rustle, the waves of the sea roar, and clouds move across the sky. These are all physical signs of the wind. So it is with the Holy Spirit. Even though He is invisible, the effects which the Holy Spirit produces can be seen and heard.

There are three places in the New Testament where we are told what happened when people were baptized in the Holy Spirit:

1. DAY OF PENTECOST:

Acts 2:2-4 is the record of what happened on the day of Pentecost:

> **And suddenly there came a sound from heaven as of a rushing mighty wind, and it filled all the house where they were sitting.**
>
> **And there appeared unto them cloven tongues like as of fire, and it sat upon each of them.**
>
> **And they were all filled with the Holy Ghost, and began to speak with other tongues, as the Spirit gave them utterance. (Acts 2:2-4)**

2. HOUSE OF CORNELIUS:

Acts 10:44-46 is the record of what happened when Peter preached the Gospel to a man named Cornelius and his family:

> **While Peter yet spoke these words, the Holy Ghost fell on all them which heard the word.**
>
> **And they of the circumcision which believed were astonished, as many as came with Peter, because that on the Gentiles also was poured out the gift of the Holy Ghost.**

For they heard them speak with tongues, and magnify God...
(Acts 10:44-46)

3. CONVERTS AT EPHESUS:

Acts 19:6 describes what happened to the first group of converts at Ephesus:

> **And when Paul had laid his hands upon them, the Holy Ghost came on them; and they spake with tongues and prophesied. (Acts 19:6)**

A COMMON SIGN: THE TONGUES

As we compare these passages there is one physical sign which is common to all three: Those who received the baptism of the Holy Spirit spoke with other tongues. Other supernatural signs of the Holy Spirit are mentioned, but none of these were evident on all three occasions.

On the day of Pentecost there was the sound of a rushing wind and visible tongues of fire were seen. These were not recorded on the other two occasions. At Ephesus the new converts prophesied. This is not mentioned as having occurred on the day of Pentecost or in the house of Cornelius.

The one outward sign which the apostles observed in the experience of Cornelius and his household was that they spoke with tongues. This physical sign was proof to the disciples that this family had been baptized in the Holy Spirit. From these Biblical records we conclude that the physical sign of speaking in tongues through the power of the Holy Spirit confirms that a person has been baptized in the Holy Spirit.

The sign of "tongues" can be languages known to man. This is what happened on the day of Pentecost:

> **...And they were all amazed and marvelled, saying one to another, Behold are not all these which speak Galilaeans?**
>
> **And how hear we every man in our own tongue, wherein we were born? (Acts 2:7-8)**

Tongues can also be a language not known to man. This is called an unknown tongue:

> **For he that speaketh in an unknown tongue speaketh not unto men, but unto God: for no man understandeth him; howbeit in the spirit he speaketh mysteries. (I Corinthians 14:2)**

PURPOSES FOR TONGUES

The sign of tongues received through baptism in the Holy Spirit has many purposes in the lives of believers. Turn to I Corinthians 14 in your Bible. These are some purposes of tongues:

-Prayer to God: Verse 2
-Self-edification: Building up yourself and increasing spiritual knowledge. Verse 4
-When interpreted they edify the church: Verses 12-13
-Intercession: Verse 14 (See also Romans 8:26-27)
-Sign to unbelievers: Verse 22
-Fulfillment of prophecy: Verse 21 (See also Isaiah 28:11-12)
-Praise: Verses 15,17

OBJECTIONS TO TONGUES

Some people object to speaking in tongues. These are some of the objections they raise:

EVERY CHRISTIAN HAS THE HOLY SPIRIT:

One of the most common objections is that every Christian receives the Holy Spirit when he is converted...He does not need any further experience to receive the baptism of the Holy Spirit. But consider the examples of people in the New Testament who were true believers. The apostles had repented of their sins and believed Jesus was the Messiah. They had witnessed personally and accepted as true the facts of His death, burial, a resurrection. Jesus told His followers:

> **And, behold, I send the promise of my Father upon you; but tarry ye in the city of Jerusalem, until ye be endued with power from on high. (Luke 24:49)**

He also said:

> **For John truly baptized with water; but ye shall be baptized with the Holy Ghost not many days hence. (Acts 1:5)**

The promised experience of being baptized in the Holy Ghost came on the day of Pentecost:

> **And they were all filled with the Holy Ghost, and began to speak with other tongues, as the Spirit gave them utterance. (Acts 2:4)**

Although the apostles were already Christians it was not until the day of Pentecost that they were filled with [baptized in] the Holy Spirit.

The people of Samaria heard the Gospel preached. They believed and were baptized in water, but they had not received the Holy Spirit:

> **Now when the apostles which were at Jerusalem heard that Samaria had received the word of God, they sent unto them Peter and John:**
>
> **Who, when they were come down, prayed for them, that they might receive the Holy Ghost:**
>
> **(For as yet he was fallen upon none of them: only they were baptized in the name of the Lord Jesus).**
>
> **Then laid they their hands on them and they received the Holy Ghost. (Acts 8:14-17)**

The people of Samaria received salvation through the ministry of Philip. They received the Holy Spirit through the ministry of Peter and John. Receiving the Holy Spirit was a separate experience from receiving salvation.

Acts 19:1-6 describes how Paul went to the city of Ephesus and met people described as "disciples." The first question Paul asked was, "Have ye received the Holy Ghost since ye believed?"

If people received the Holy Ghost when they received salvation it would be foolish for Paul to ask this question. The fact that he asked it makes it clear that people become believers without receiving the baptism of the Holy Spirit. Even if a person receives the baptism of the Holy Spirit at the same time he is converted, it is still a separate experience from salvation.

As you previously learned, the ministry of the Holy Spirit can be observed from the very creation of the world. The Old Testament speaks of the Holy Spirit coming on Israel's spiritual leaders. The Holy Spirit is also operative in the life of a sinner to bring him to Christ.

But these ministries of the Holy Spirit are different from being baptized with the Holy Spirit. Jesus made that clear when He said:

> **Even the Spirit of truth; whom the world cannot receive, because it seeth Him not, neither knoweth him: but ye know Him: for He dwelleth with you [presently], and shall be in you [in the future]. (John 14:17)**

The Holy Spirit was with the disciples at that time, but not yet in them. They were filled [baptized] with the Holy Spirit on the Day of Pentecost.

The Holy Spirit is WITH the sinner to draw him to Jesus Christ. But this is not the same as being IN him.

In Old Testament times the power of the Holy Spirit came upon spiritual leaders at special times. In the New Testament this power was given permanently to believers.

The Holy Spirit was WITH the spiritual leaders of Old Testament times. But He was not yet IN them. This is the difference between the Old and New Testament ministries of the Holy Spirit.

DO ALL SPEAK WITH TONGUES?

Another objection to tongues has come through misunderstanding of a question of the Apostle Paul. In I Corinthians 12:30 he asks, "Do all speak with tongues?" The answer to his question is "No, all do not speak with tongues." But Paul is not speaking here of the experience of being baptized in the Holy Spirit. The discussion concerns gifts of the Holy Spirit which can be used by the believer in the church.

> **Now ye are the body of Christ, and members in particular.**
>
> **And God hath set some in the church, first apostles, secondarily prophets, thirdly teachers, after that miracles, then gifts of healings, helps, governments, diversities of tongues. (I Corinthians 12:27-28)**

Paul is speaking of gifts which may be used by members of the church. One of the gifts of the Holy Spirit is "diversitics of tongues." It is an ability to give special messages to the church in tongues through the power of the Holy Spirit.

Although everyone experiences the sign of tongues when baptized in the Holy Spirit, not everyone receives the special gift of diversities of tongues. (This subject is discussed further in Chapter Nine).

FEAR:

Some believers do not seek the baptism of the Holy Spirit because they arc afraid they will receive an experience that is not of God. But the Bible says:

> **Ask, and it shall be given you; seek and ye shall find; knock, and it shall be opened unto you;**
>
> **For every one that asketh receiveth; and he that seeketh findeth; and to him that knocketh it shall be opened.**

> **Or what man is there of you whom if his son ask bread, will he give him a stone?**
>
> **Or if he ask a fish, will he give him a serpent?**
>
> **If ye then being evil, know how to give good gifts unto your children, how much more shall your Father which is in heaven give good things to them that ask Him? (Matthew 7:7-11)**

If a believer asks God for something, just like a good earthly Father, God will not let him receive anything that will harm him.

EMOTIONAL EXPERIENCE:

Another objection to tongues is that it is an emotional experience. Many believers who receive the baptism of the Holy Spirit emphasize their own emotional reactions to the experience.

Man is an emotional creature. Conversion to Jesus Christ does not eliminate a man's emotions. He will still experience joy and sorrow. Conversion frees man's emotions from the control of sin. It redirects these emotions to worship of God.

The word "joy" in Scripture is closely associated with the Holy Spirit. In Acts 13:52 we read that "the disciples were filled with joy, and with the Holy Ghost." Some people react with great emotion to the joy which comes with the baptism of the Holy Spirit because they are naturally more emotional than others. They may shout, laugh, or experience sensations in their physical bodies.

But these emotional reactions are not the sign of baptism in the Holy Spirit. The confirming sign is speaking in tongues. The evidence is power. It is not necessary to show great emotion such as laughing, shouting, dancing, etc., to be baptized in the Holy Spirit. How one reacts emotionally to the joy this experience brings is often related to his individual emotions.

But you should not criticize those who have joyful, emotional reactions to the Holy Spirit. The Bible records emotional reactions of those who had a powerful experience with God. People trembled, fell prostrate on the ground, shouted, rejoiced, and danced before God.

It is interesting to observe the emotional reaction of people to various athletic events. They will yell, laugh, jump up and down, and express much excitement over a sports game. How much more excited we should be over a gift like the Holy Spirit which accomplishes so many purposes in our lives, brings great joy, and equips us with power to reach the world with the Gospel.

The Psalmist David agreed. He presents a picture of joyful, loud, emotional worship of God:

O come, let us sing unto the Lord: let us make a joyful noise to the rock of our salvation.

Let us come before His presence with thanksgiving, and make a joyful noise unto Him with psalms.

For the Lord is a great God, and a great King above all gods. (Psalms 95:1-3)

Praise Him with the sound of the trumpet; praise Him with the psaltery and harp.

Praise Him with the timbrel and dance; praise Him with stringed instruments and organs.

Praise Him upon the loud cymbals; praise Him upon the high sounding cymbals.

Let every thing that hath breath praise the Lord. Praise ye the Lord. (Psalms 150:3-6)

You do not have to fear that the baptism in the Holy Spirit will cause you to do something improper or lose control of yourself.

Paul said there were times to "keep silent" and "hold your peace" in regards to speaking in tongues (I Corinthians 14). He would not make these statements if the Holy Spirit caused people to be out of control. The Bible says:

And the spirits of the prophets are subject to the prophets. (I Corinthians 14:32)

This means that any gift God gives is subject to or under the control of the user. God does nothing improper for...

...God is not the author of confusion, but of peace...(I Corinthians 14:33)

RECEIVING THE HOLY SPIRIT

The following are guidelines for receiving the baptism of the Holy Spirit.

REPENT AND BE BAPTIZED:

> **Then Peter said unto them, Repent, and be baptized every one of you in the name of Jesus Christ for the remission of sins, and ye shall receive the gift of the Holy Ghost. (Acts 2:38)**

BELIEVE IT IS FOR YOU:

> **For the promise is unto you, and to your children, and to all that are afar off, even as many as the Lord our God shall call. (Acts 2:39)**

DESIRE IT:

> **...Jesus stood and cried, saying, if any man thirst let him come unto me, and drink.**
>
> **He that believeth on me, as the scripture hath said, out of his belly shall flow rivers of living water.**
>
> **(but this spake He of the Spirit, which they that believed on Him should receive; for the Holy Ghost was not yet given; because that Jesus was not yet glorified.) (John 7:37-39)**

ACCEPT IT AS A GIFT:

The Holy Spirit has already been given. It was given to the Church on the Day of Pentecost. Because it is a gift, you can do nothing to earn it:

> **...the gift of the Holy Ghost. (Acts 2:38)**
>
> **This only would I learn of you. Received ye the Spirit by the works of the law, or by the hearing of faith?**
>
> **He therefore that ministereth to you in the Spirit, and worketh miracles among you, doeth he it by the works of the law, or by the hearing of faith?**
>
> **That the blessing of Abraham might come on the Gentiles; through Jesus Christ; that we might receive the promise of the Spirit through faith. (Galatians 3:2,5,14)**

Begin to praise and thank God for the gift of the Holy Spirit.

YIELD TO GOD:

Yield your tongue to God in praise and worship. As you praise Him audibly you may first experience stammering lips. As you continue to yield your tongue to the Holy Spirit and He will speak through you words foreign to your understanding. This is the confirming physical sign of Holy Spirit baptism:

> **For with stammering lips and another tongue will he speak to this people. (Isaiah 28:11)**
>
> **And they were all filled with the Holy Ghost, and began to speak with other tongues, as the Spirit gave them utterance. (Acts 2:4)**

REQUEST THE PRAYERS OF OTHER BELIEVERS:

The Holy Spirit can be received through the laying on of hands (Acts 8,9,19) or without the laying on of hands (Acts 2,4,10). Study these chapters which show how Spirit-filled believers can help you experience baptism in the Holy Spirit.

IMPORTANCE OF THE EXPERIENCE

Baptism in the Holy Spirit is important because it enables you to become a powerful witness of the Gospel message:

> **But ye shall receive power after that the Holy Ghost is come upon you: and ye shall be witnesses unto me, both in Jerusalem, and in all Judaea, and in Samaria, and unto the uttermost part of the earth. (Acts 1:8)**
>
> **And these signs shall follow them that believe; In my name shall they cast out devils; they shall speak with new tongues;**
>
> **They shall take up serpents; and if they drink any deadly thing, it shall not hurt them; they shall lay hands on the sick and they shall recover. (Mark 16:17-18)**

The Holy Spirit also gives special spiritual gifts and develops spiritual fruit in your life. These gifts and fruit are the subject of the remaining chapters of this study.

SELF-TEST

1. Write the Key Verse from memory.

____

2. Give six guidelines for receiving the Baptism of the Holy Spirit.

_______________ _______________ _______________

_______________ _______________ _______________

3. What is the outward physical sign of the baptism of the Holy Spirit?

____

4. What is the true evidence of baptism in the Holy Spirit. Give a Biblical reference to support your answer.

____

5. What are the four main objections some people have to the sign of "other tongues"?

_______________ _______________

_______________ _______________

6. Are any of these objections valid on the basis of Scripture?_______________

7. What is the meaning of the word "baptize"?

____

8. List three Scripture references where we are told what happened when people received the baptism of the Holy Ghost.

_______________ _______________ _______________

(Answers to tests are provided at the conclusion of the final chapter in this manual.)

FOR FURTHER STUDY

1. The Holy Spirit is mentioned 85 times in the Old Testament. As you read the Old Testament circle each mention of the Holy Spirit. This study will help you understand His ministry before New Testament times. If you completed the similar assignment for the New Testament given in Chapter Two, you will have a complete study of the Holy Spirit marked right in your own Bible.

2. The gift of the Holy Spirit was given as a fulfillment of promises which dated back to Old Testament times. Study these promises of the Holy Spirit:

   Old Testament:

   Isaiah 28:11-12
   Joel 2:28-29
   Isaiah 44:3

   New Testament:

   John 7:38-39; 14:16-18; 15:26; 16:7-11
   Acts 1:4,5,8; 2:38-39
   Galatians 3:14
   Luke 24:49

3. Have you experienced the baptism of the Holy Spirit? If not, follow the guidelines given in this chapter to receive it.

4. Review the purposes for tongues discussed in this chapter. Which of these purposes have you witnessed in the use of other tongues?

5. Review the objections to speaking in tongues which were discussed in this lesson. Think about how you will respond the next time you hear one of these objections raised.

CHAPTER FIVE

INTRODUCTION TO THE GIFTS OF THE HOLY SPIRIT

OBJECTIVES:

Upon completion of this chapter you will be able to:

- Define spiritual gifts.
- Identify the source of these gifts.
- Distinguish between spiritual gifts and natural talents.
- Explain purposes for spiritual gifts.
- Explain the objectives of spiritual gifts.
- Explain how these gifts are distributed.
- Identify abuses of spiritual gifts.
- Identify the key to using spiritual gifts.
- Distinguish between true and false [counterfeit] spiritual gifts.

KEY VERSE:

> **Now concerning spiritual gifts, brethren, I would not have you ignorant. (I Corinthians 12:1)**

INTRODUCTION

Jesus left His followers with the responsibility to extend the Gospel message to the ends of the earth. The power of the Holy Spirit would help them fulfill this task:

> **But ye shall receive power after that the Holy Ghost is come upon you: and ye shall be witnesses unto me both in Jerusalem and in all Judaea, and in Samaria, and unto the uttermost part of the earth. (Acts 1:8)**

Jesus did not leave His followers with such a great responsibility without giving them the ability to fulfill the challenge. Spiritual gifts are supernatural abilities given by the Holy Spirit to empower believers to be effective witnesses of the Gospel.

The subject of spiritual gifts was one on which Paul taught in the early church. He said:

Now concerning spiritual gifts , brethren, I would not have you ignorant. (I Corinthians 12:1)

This chapter introduces the subject of spiritual gifts. Following chapters will concern the various spiritual gifts available to believers. Guidelines also will be given to help you discover your own spiritual gift.

WHAT ARE SPIRITUAL GIFTS?

The word "spiritual" means "characterized or controlled by the Holy Spirit." A "gift" is something freely given from one person to another. A spiritual gift is a supernatural ability given by the Holy Spirit to a believer to minister as part of the Body of Christ.

There is a difference between the "gift" of the Holy Spirit and "gifts" of the Holy Spirit. The "gift" of the Holy Spirit occurred at Pentecost (Acts 2) when the Holy Spirit came in answer to the promise of Jesus:

And I will pray the Father, and He shall give you another Comforter...Even the Spirit of truth...(John 14:16-17a)

The "gift" of the Holy Spirit has already been given in answer to this promise. "Gifts" of the Holy Spirit are supernatural abilities the Holy Spirit gives believers to enable effective ministry:

And they went forth, and preached every where, the Lord working with them, and confirming the word with signs following. (Mark 16:20)

GIFTS AND TALENTS

There is a difference between spiritual gifts and natural talents. A talent is a natural ability inherited at birth or developed through training. A spiritual gift is a supernatural ability which did not come by inheritance or training. It is a special ability given by the Holy Spirit to be used for specific spiritual purposes.

It is possible that a natural talent may be sanctioned [approved and blessed] by the Holy Spirit after one becomes a believer. When this occurs the talent then becomes a gift as well as a talent. For example, a person may have a natural talent in administration because of training he has received. After baptism in the Holy Spirit this natural talent may be sanctioned [approved] by the Holy Spirit and he may be used in the spiritual gift of administration.

Spiritual gifts provide spiritual capabilities far greater than the finest natural talents. Although we should use all our natural talents for the work of the Lord, we still need spiritual gifts.

PURPOSES OF THE GIFTS

The purposes of the gifts of the Holy Spirit are listed in Ephesians 4:12-15:

> **For the perfecting of the saints, for the work of the ministry, for the edifying of the body of Christ;**
>
> **Till we all come in the unity of the faith, and of the knowledge of the Son of God, unto a perfect man, unto the measure of the stature of the fulness of Christ:**
>
> **That we henceforth be no more children, tossed to and fro, and carried about with every wind of doctrine by the slight of men, and cunning craftiness, whereby they lie in wait to deceive;**
>
> **But speaking the truth in love, may grow up into Him in all things, which is the head, even Christ. (Ephesians 4:12-15)**

According to this passage, the purposes of the Holy Spirit are to:

-Perfect the saints
-Promote the work of the ministry
-Edify Christ and the Church

The objectives or goals of spiritual gifts are that we will:

-Become united in the faith.
-Develop our knowledge of Christ.
-Develop in perfection, with Christ as our model.
-Become stable, not deceived by false doctrines.
-Mature spiritually in Christ.

THE TRINITY AND THE GIFTS

You learned earlier that the Holy Spirit is part of the Trinity of God. All three persons of the Trinity are involved in empowering believers with spiritual gifts:

> **Now there are diversities of gifts, but the same Spirit. And there are differences of administrations, but the same Lord. And there are diversities of operations, but it is the same God which worketh all in all.**
> **(I Corinthians 12:4-6)**

The Holy Spirit, God, and the Lord [Jesus Christ] are all mentioned in this passage. Their involvement in spiritual gifts is shown in the following chart:

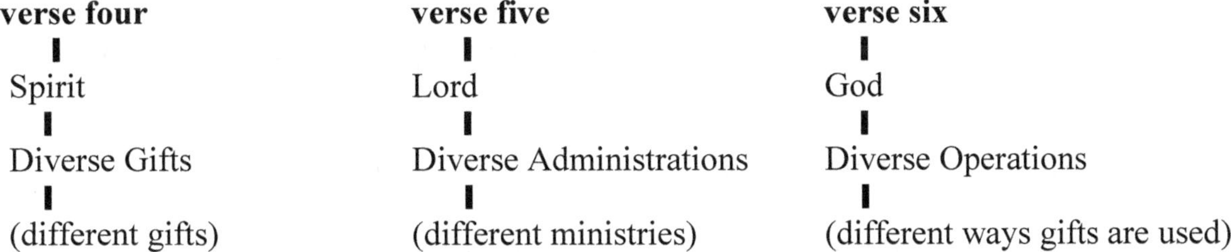

SPIRITUAL WEAPONS

The gifts of the Spirit are also given to the Church as weapons of spiritual warfare to conquer the spiritual forces of Satan:*

> **For we wrestle not against flesh and blood, but against principalities, against powers, against the rulers of the darkness of this world, against spiritual wickedness in high places. (Ephesians 6:12)**

Since the battle in which believers are engaged is spiritual, then spiritual rather than natural weapons must be used. Believers sometimes go into spiritual warfare without knowledge of these weapons. Anytime you go to battle without your weapons you cannot expect to win the fight. This is why it is important to understand spiritual gifts. They are part of the spiritual weapons God has provided.

DISTRIBUTION OF THE GIFTS

Each believer has at least one spiritual gift:

> **As every man hath received the gift, even so minister the same one to another, as good stewards of the manifold grace of God. (I Peter 4:10)**
>
> **But the manifestation of the Spirit is given to every man to profit withal.**
>
> **But all these worketh that one and the selfsame Spirit, dividing to every man severally as He will. (I Corinthians 12:7,11)**

---

* Harvestime offers a separate course on the subject of spiritual warfare entitled *"Spiritual Strategies: A Manual Of Spiritual Warfare."*

Because every believer has at least one spiritual gift, we each have a responsibility to discover and use our gift.

You will not be judged by how many spiritual gifts you have. You will be judged by your faithfulness to use the spiritual gift or gifts you have been given. The parable of the talents in Matthew 25:14-30 confirms this truth.

There are many spiritual gifts, but no believer has all of the gifts of the Holy Spirit:

> **Are all apostles? are all prophets? are all teachers? are all workers of miracles?**
>
> **Have all the gifts of healing? do all speak with tongues? do all interpret? (I Corinthians 12:29-30)**

A person may have more than one gift, but no one has all the gifts of the Spirit. If he did, then he would have no need of others in the Body of Christ.

THE ABUSE OF GIFTS

A spiritual gift from God can be abused. To "abuse" a gift means to not use it properly. You can abuse spiritual gifts by:

NOT USING GIFTS GIVEN TO YOU:

The Apostle Paul told Timothy:

> **Neglect not the gift that is in thee, which was given thee by prophecy, with the laying on of the hands of the presbytery. (I Timothy 4:14)**
>
> **Wherefore I put thee in remembrance that thou stir up the gift of God, which is in thee by the putting on of my hands. (II Timothy 1:6)**

ATTEMPTING TO USE GIFTS NOT GIVEN TO YOU:

While ministering in Samaria, Peter and John met a man named Simon who wanted to have the powerful gifts he saw demonstrated. Simon offered money to obtain these abilities. Peter said:

> **Thy money perish with thee, because thou hast thought that the gift of God may be purchased with money. Thou hast neither part nor lot in this matter... (Acts 8:20-21)**

Spiritual gifts come from the Holy Spirit. They cannot be obtained by any other method. You cannot just decide you want to have or use a certain spiritual gift. The Holy Spirit must give it to you.

On another occasion, seven sons of the chief of the priests saw the miracles of the Apostle Paul and tried to use this gift to cast out evil spirits:

> **And the evil spirit answered and said, Jesus I know, and Paul I know; but who are ye?**
>
> **And the man in whom the evil spirit was leaped on them and overcame them, and prevailed against them so that they fled out of that house naked and wounded. (Acts 19:15-16)**

It can be dangerous to try to operate a gift without the Holy Spirit's anointing.

NOT USING THE GIFTS PROPERLY:

In I Corinthians 12-14 Paul deals with proper use of spiritual gifts. To summarize the teaching of these chapters he states:

> **For God is not the author of confusion, but of peace...Let all things be done decently and in order. (I Corinthians 14:33,40)**

God is not the author of confusion. Where there is confusion the gifts are not being used correctly. Spiritual gifts can also be improperly used when you manipulate people, gain wealth, or use them for your own selfish satisfaction rather than in ministry to others.

The guidelines for use of gifts which Paul gives in I Corinthians 12-14 prevent confusion. You will have an opportunity to study these in the "For Further Study" section of this lesson.

GLORIYING YOUR GIFT:

When you "glorify" your gift, you consider it more special than other gifts. You begin to see the gift as greater than the Giver.

MANY GIFTS FROM ONE SOURCE

The Bible indicates there are many gifts which come from one source. The source of spiritual gifts is the Holy Spirit. He gives and operates these gifts in the lives of believers:

Now there are diversities of gifts, but the same Spirit.

And there are differences of administrations, but the same Lord.

And there are diversities of operations, but it is the same God which worketh all in all.

But the manifestation of the Spirit is given to every man to profit withal. (I Corinthians 12:4-7)

Having then gifts differing according to the grace that is given to us, whether prophecy, let us prophesy according to the proportion of faith;

Or ministry, let us wait on our ministering; or he that teacheth on teaching;

Or he that exhorteth on exhortation: he that giveth let him do it with simplicity; he that ruleth with diligence; he that showeth mercy, with cheerfulness. (Romans 12:6-8)

There is one source of spiritual gifts but there are many different gifts. No gift is more important than another. Your position in the Body of Christ is compared to parts of a human body. Just as in the human body, the smaller parts such as the eye have important functions, the seemingly "small" gift is often quite important in the functioning of the church. Some gifts involve greater responsibilities, but no gift is more important than another.

Some parts of the human body have greater responsibilities than others. For example, the eye lets you see what is around you. It guides you when walking. It permits you to read and see and enjoy God's creations. The eye has greater responsibility, but it is no more important than the big toe which provides balance for walking. The guidance of the eye for walking is useless if you have no feet with which to walk. The eye's function to permit reading is useless if you have no brain to understand what you read.

Sometimes misunderstanding arises in the Church when believers do not recognize the spiritual gifts of others. For example, one person may have the gift of giving and may not understand another believer who does not give as liberally. Or one may have the gift of administration and become very impatient with people who are less organized.

Each believer should use his spiritual gifts to work together with other believers who have different gifts. When this happens, the Church functions effectively as the Body of Christ.

STEWARDS OF GIFTS

You are only a steward of spiritual gifts. A steward is someone who does not own that with which he works. He uses something given to him by another person. He uses it in behalf of the person who gave it to him. You are a steward for Jesus Christ:

> **Let a man so account of us, as of the ministers of Christ, and stewards of the mysteries of God. (I Corinthians 4:1)**

Part of the "mysteries" of which you are a steward are spiritual gifts. They are given to you by the Holy Spirit to minister effectively for Jesus:

> **As every man hath received the gift, even so minister the same one to another, as good stewards of the manifold grace of God. (I Peter 4:10)**

As a steward, you will be judged on the basis of your faithfulness to use the gifts you have been given:

> **Moreover it is required in stewards, that a man be found faithful. (I Corinthians 4:2)**

THE GIFTS OF THE SPIRIT

The main passages identifying spiritual gifts are listed below. Read these before you study the following chapters. These verses introduce the various gifts:

-Romans 12:1-8
-Ephesians 4:1-16
-I Corinthians 12:1-31
-I Peter 4:7-11

Remember that these gifts are special abilities from God to minister in different ways. While there may be some evidences of these in all our lives it does not necessarily mean we have a certain gift. For example, all believers are to give to the work of the Lord with tithes and offerings. But the gift of giving is an unusual generosity prompted by the Spirit of God. All believers have a measure of faith according to the Word of God. But the gift of faith is a special ability to believe beyond that of the ordinary Christian.

ARE GIFTS FOR TODAY?

Some people claim that all of the spiritual gifts listed in the Bible are not for the Church today. They believe some gifts, like prophecy, tongues, miracles, etc., were only for the early Church. These people say that after the Church was established and the New Testament written, some spiritual gifts were no longer needed. They often use I Corinthians 13:10 to explain their belief:

> **But when that which is perfect is come, then that which is in part shall be done away. (I Corinthians 13:10)**

They say that when the perfect revelation of God's Word was written, there was no longer a need for tongues, interpretation, and prophecy. They say that once the Church was established there was no longer a need for confirming signs and miracles.

What they fail to note is that knowledge is also mentioned in the same passage as being "vanished" or done away with:

> **...whether there be prophecies, they shall fail; whether there be tongues, they shall cease; whether there be knowledge, it shall vanish away.**
> **(I Corinthians 13:8)**

If we use this verse to say tongues, interpretation, and prophecy are no longer needed, then we must also say knowledge is no longer needed.

This passage actually refers to a future time when the "perfect" Kingdom of God is established on earth. Since what is perfect has come, we will have no need of any of the spiritual gifts then, because...

> **...He will dwell with them, and they shall be His people, and God Himself shall be with them, and be their God. (Revelation 21:3)**

We will have no need of messages through prophecy, tongues, or interpretation, for we will be dwelling with the God who inspires such messages. We will have no need of the word of wisdom or knowledge, for we will be living with the source of knowledge. We will not need discerning of spirits, for...

> **...there shall no wise enter into it any thing that defileth...but they which are written in the Lamb's book of life. (Revelation 21:27)**

There will be no need for gifts of healing for...

> **...In the midst of the street of it, and on either side of the river, was there the tree of life...for the healing of the nations. (Revelation 22:2)**

Also remember the purposes and objectives of spiritual gifts given in Ephesians 4:12-15. The purposes are for:

-Perfecting of the saints.
-Promoting the work of the ministry.
-Edifying Christ and the Church.

The purposes for which the gifts were given still remain. The saints still need to be perfected, the ministry still needs to be promoted to the ends of the earth, and Christ and the Church need to be edified.

The objectives are that we will:

-Be united in the faith.
-Develop our knowledge of Christ.
-Develop in perfection, with Christ as our model.
-Become stable, not deceived by false doctrines.
-Mature spiritually in Christ.

God would not give spiritual gifts for these purposes and objectives and then remove them without these things being accomplished.

-Are all believers united in the faith?
-Has everyone developed fully in the knowledge of Christ?
-Are we all perfected?
-Are our church members stable and not being deceived by false doctrines?
-Are all our church members spiritually mature?

The answer to all these questions is "no." These objectives have not been accomplished. For this reason we know all of the spiritual gifts are still for today. God gave spiritual gifts to accomplish certain purposes in the Church. He will not withdraw any of these gifts without these purposes being accomplished. The Bible also says that the "gifts and callings of God are without repentance" (Romans 11:29). This means God will not change His mind and take back a spiritual gift or calling He has given.

THE KEY TO USING GIFTS

In I Corinthians 13 the Apostle Paul gives the key for using gifts of the Holy Spirit. He introduced the subject in I Corinthians 12:31. He listed some of the gifts of the Holy Spirit and then said...

...and yet shew I unto you a more excellent way. (I Corinthians 12:31)

I Corinthians chapter 13 explains that "more excellent way." Read the entire chapter in your Bible. This chapter gives the key to using spiritual gifts. That key is love. You can prophesy, have the gifts of healing, faith, giving, etc., but without love in using these gifts, they will not be effective.

Gifts are unprofitable when used without love. Speaking in tongues becomes like a noisy clanging. Every gift is worthless, "it profits nothing", unless it is used in love. Love is the "more excellent way" in which the gifts are used. The gifts become a channel through which God's love can flow to those around us. Love is the key to using spiritual gifts effectively.

A WARNING: SATAN'S COUNTERFEIT

Satan counterfeits the gifts of the Holy Spirit. A counterfeit is something that imitates something real, but it is not genuine. Satan is a deceiver. The Bible says he sometimes even appears as an angel (II Corinthians 11:14). In the final days of time, there will even be a Satanic counterfeit of Christ called the antichrist (I John 2:18,22).

Much counterfeiting of the gifts is accomplished through the occult. For example, the word of knowledge is counterfeited by witches pretending to foretell the future and the unknown. A witch is a person who seeks to know things and perform acts through supernatural sources other than God. Their source is Satan. Counterfeiting of the gift of discerning of spirits is done by mind reading.

Even miracles are counterfeited by Satan (Exodus 7) and will be performed by the antichrist (Revelation 13:14). The Bible also speaks of false prophets (Acts 13:6-12). The question is, how do you distinguish the counterfeit from the real?

The counterfeit does not fulfill the Scriptural purposes of the gifts of the Holy Spirit. Read again Ephesians 4:12-15. Any true gift of the Holy Spirit will accomplish these spiritual purposes and objectives.

Counterfeit gifts do not agree with what the Bible teaches about Jesus. When anyone ministers a gift, what do they say about Jesus? Does it agree with the written Word of God?

> **But I fear, lest by any means, as the serpent beguiled Eve through his subtilty, so your minds should be corrupted from the simplicity that is in Christ.**
>
> **For if he that cometh preacheth another Jesus, whom we have not preached, or if ye receive another spirit, which ye have not received, or another gospel, which ye have not accepted, ye might well bear with him.**
> **(II Corinthians 11:3-4)**

You can also recognize counterfeiters by their personal characteristics. These are listed in II Peter 2 and the book of Jude. Study these chapters in your Bible to help you distinguish the real from the counterfeit.

SELF-TEST

1. Write the Key Verse from memory.

____

____

2. What is the difference between spiritual gifts and natural talents?

____

3. List the three purposes for spiritual gifts:

_______________ _______________ _______________

4. List five objectives for spiritual gifts:

__________ __________ __________ __________ __________

5. Does everyone have at least one spiritual gift? Give at least one Scriptural reference to support your answer.

____

6. List four abuses of spiritual gifts:

__________ __________ __________ __________

7. Who is the source of spiritual gifts?______________________________

8. What is the key to using your spiritual gift?______________________

9. How can you distinguish the real gifts of the Holy Spirit from Satan's counterfeit?

____

10. What are spiritual gifts?

____

11. Are all the spiritual gifts for today, or were some just for the early Church? Explain your answer.

____

12. What is the difference between spiritual "gifts" and the "gift" of the Holy Spirit?

____

13. Read each statement. If the statement is TRUE write T on the blank in front of it. If the statement is FALSE write F on the blank in front of it.

a.______Human talents are not spiritual gifts.

b.______You are born with spiritual gifts.

c.______God gives spiritual gifts especially for your own pleasure.

d.______Since the church is firmly established, supernatural signs of God's power are no longer for today.

e.______"That which is perfect" is already here so we no longer need tongues, interpretation, and prophecy.

f.______No one Christian has all the gifts.

g.______We cannot choose our gifts.

h.______We will have to give an account to God for the way in which we use our gifts.

i.______Gifts used without love are not effective.

(Answers to tests are provided at the conclusion of the final chapter in this manual.)

FOR FURTHER STUDY

1. Study II Peter 2 and the book of Jude. List the personal characteristics of "false prophets" and "certain men who crept in unawares." These are people who are counterfeits. They are not true believers and use false gifts to deceive God's people.

2. Natural talents can be used by God as well as spiritual gifts. Look up the following verses. List the names of the individuals and their natural talent:

NATURAL TALENTS

Reference	**Name**	**Talent**
Genesis 4:20	____________________	____________________
Genesis 4:2	____________________	____________________
Genesis 4:21	____________________	____________________
Genesis 4:22	____________________	____________________
Genesis 25:27	____________________	____________________

3. Study the following references and complete the sentences.

   It is important to know about spiritual gifts because:

   a. We will be held ____________________ to God for their use.

      We are a ______________________.

      (I Peter 4:10; I Corinthians 4:1-2; Matthew 25:14-30)

   b. We are to be ____________________ of them and _____________ them.

      (I Timothy 4:14; I Corinthians 12:1)

4. I Corinthians 13 lists many qualities of love. Write the verse number which mentions each quality in the blanks provided. The first one is done as an example for you to follow:

__5__Patient
_____Kind
_____Not jealous
_____Does not brag
_____Not arrogant
_____Does not act unbecomingly
_____Does not seek its own
_____Not provoked
_____Does not take into account a wrong suffered
_____Does not rejoice in unrighteousness
_____Rejoices with the truth
_____Bears all things
_____Believes all things
_____Hopes all things
_____Endures all things

Write down the name of someone you have difficulty in loving. Look over the qualities listed above. List the specific qualities of love you will need in order to love this person.

I have difficulty in loving_______________.

I will need these following specific qualities in order to love him/her:

____

5. Use the following outline to study the proper use of gifts as discussed by Paul in I Corinthians 12-14.

I. You should have knowledge of spiritual gifts: I Corinthians 12:1

II. There are many gifts but they all come from the same Spirit: The Trinity of God is at work in all of the gifts. I Corinthians 12:4-11

III. We are to function as a body in using spiritual gifts: Each part should be in harmony with other parts. I Corinthians 12:12-31

A. There should be no division [schism] in the body. We should all care for each other: I Corinthians 12:25-26
B. God sets spiritual gifts in order in the church: I Corinthians 12:28

C. Not everyone has the same gift: I Corinthians 12:28-30

D. We should desire spiritual gifts. I Corinthians 12:31; 14:1

E. Love is the key to using all gifts: I Corinthians 13

F. Gifts should edify the church: I Corinthians 14:12

IV. If you have the gift of tongues you should also pray for the gift of interpretation: I Corinthians 14:1-13

A. Praising in the Spirit without understanding and praising with understanding are both part of worship: I Corinthians 14:14-15

B. Speaking words that others understand is important when there are unbelievers present: I Corinthians 14:16-19

C. Tongues are a sign to those who do not believe: I Corinthians 14:22-25

D. Prophesying benefits those who believe: I Corinthians 14:22-25

V. All things should be done in an orderly way during worship services. Tongues should not be used unless there is someone present with the gift of interpretation: I Corinthians 14:26-31

A. You do not lose control when the Holy Spirit ministers through you. You have the control to use the gifts properly: I Corinthians 14:32

B. Confusion is not of God: I Corinthians 14:33

VI. You should not forbid to speak in tongues and you should desire to prophesy: I Corinthians 14:39

VII. Foolish questioning should not be part of the worship service: I Corinthians 14:34-35,37-38

VIII. The main guideline for proper use of gifts: Let all things be done decently and in order. I Corinthians 14:40

CHAPTER SIX

SPECIAL GIFTS OF THE HOLY SPIRIT

OBJECTIVES:

Upon completion of this chapter you will be able to:

- Name four divisions of spiritual gifts used in this study.
- Identify the special gifts of the Holy Spirit.
- Explain the difference between the special gift of being a prophet and the gift of prophecy.
- Explain the difference between the special gift of being a teacher and the gift of teaching.

KEY VERSE:

> **And He gave some apostles; and some prophets; and some, evangelists, and some pastors and teachers. (Ephesians 4:11)**

INTRODUCTION

Before studying this chapter read the Bible passages below. These references list the gifts of the Holy Spirit:

-Romans 12:1-8
-I Corinthians 12:1-31
-Ephesians 4:1-16
-I Peter 4:7-11

Turn to the Appendix of this manual. Read these same passages as they are translated in the Amplified version of the Bible. For study purposes we have divided the gifts into four major categories:

-Special Gifts
-Speaking Gifts
-Serving Gifts
-Sign Gifts

The Bible does not make such a division of the gifts. We have made it to help you remember the various gifts more easily. This chapter discusses the special gifts. Following chapters explain speaking, serving, and sign gifts.

SET IN THE BODY

The previous chapter explained the unity and diversity of spiritual gifts. Although there are many different gifts, they all come from one source. That source is the Holy Spirit. God has a specific place in the Church for each believer:

> **But now hath God set the members, every one of them, in the body, as it hath pleased Him. (I Corinthians 12:18)**

Every member has a place which God has chosen for him. He is equipped to fulfill his special purpose in the church through the gifts of the Holy Spirit.

When each believer is filling the place God has chosen for him and using his spiritual gift, the church operates smoothly. God compares it to the operation of the human body in which each member...from the eye to the toe...knows and performs its function (I Corinthians 12:1-31). Remember as you study these spiritual gifts that each is equally important in the Body of Christ just as each member of the human body is important:

> **And the eye cannot say unto the hand, I have no need of thee: nor again the head to the feet, I have no need of you.**
>
> **Nay, much more those members of the body, which seem to be more feeble, are necessary. (I Corinthians 12:21-22)**

As you study spiritual gifts, remember also that they are not natural abilities. They are abilities from the Holy Spirit to equip believers for Christian service.

(Note: In this and the following three chapters suggestions are given "For Further Study" as each spiritual gift is discussed. This is done to permit you to complete your study of each gift before going on to the next one.)

SPECIAL GIFTS

The first group of spiritual gifts are what we will call "special gifts." We use this title for these gifts because each one is a special leadership position in the church:

> **And He gave some, apostles; and some, prophets, and some, evangelists; and some, pastors and teachers. (Ephesians 4:11)**

These leadership positions are sometimes called "offices" in the church. "Office" means a place of responsibility and duty. The special leadership gifts are:

-Apostles
-Prophets
-Evangelists
-Pastors
-Teachers

APOSTLES

And God hath set some in the church, first apostles, secondarily prophets... (I Corinthians 12:28)

And He gave some apostles; and some, prophets... (Ephesians 4:11)

An apostle is one who has a special ability to develop new churches in different places and cultures and to oversee a number of churches as a supervisor. Apostle means "a delegate, one sent with full power and authority to act for another." The apostle has a special authority or ability to extend the Gospel throughout the world by developing organized bodies of believers. Modern terms used by the church for an apostle are missionary and church-planter.

The Bible speaks of three different categories of apostles. Jesus Christ was called an apostle:

Wherefore holy brethren, partakers of the heavenly calling, consider the Apostle and High Priest of our profession, Christ Jesus;

Who was faithful to Him that appointed Him... (Hebrews 3:1-2a)

The twelve disciples of Jesus were called apostles:

Now the names of the twelve apostles are these... (Matthew 10:2)

The twelve apostles had a special function. They were part of the founding of the Church. While they had a function which no other believers will ever have, there is also a general apostolic gift of the Holy Spirit:

And He gave some apostles... (Ephesians 4:11)

According to this passage, God is the one who selects apostles. Paul again confirms this:

And God hath set some in the church, first apostles... (I Corinthians 12:28)

The Bible speaks of special signs which confirm that a person has the gift of being an apostle:

> **Truly the signs of an apostle were wrought among you in all patience, in signs, and wonders, and mighty deeds. (II Corinthians 12:12)**
>
> **And by the hands of the apostles were many signs and wonders wrought among the people... (Acts 5:12)**

The special leadership of apostles over the churches is illustrated in the book of Acts:

> **And certain men which came down from Judaea taught the brethren and said, Except ye be circumcised after the manner of Moses, ye cannot be saved.**
>
> **When therefore Paul and Barnabas had no small dissension and disputation with them, they determined that Paul and Barnabas, and certain other of them, should go up to Jerusalem unto the apostles and elders about this question. (Acts 15:1-2)**
>
> **And as they went through the cities, they delivered them the decrees for to keep, that were ordained of the apostles and elders which were at Jerusalem.**
>
> **And so were the churches established in the faith, and increased in number daily. (Acts 16:4-5)**

Apostles extend the Gospel message by raising up churches. They give leadership to these churches and have special spiritual signs in their ministry. The calling and desire to be an apostle comes from God:

> **Paul, an apostle, (not of men, neither by man, but by Jesus Christ, and God the Father, who raised him from the dead. (Galatians 1:1)**

This special gift is usually recognized by a local church who does the sending of the apostle to other places:

> **Now there were in the church that was at Antioch, certain prophets and teachers...**
>
> **As they ministered to the Lord, and fasted, the Holy Ghost said, Separate me Barnabas and Saul for the work whereunto I have called them.**

And when they had fasted and prayed, and laid their hands on them, they sent them away. (Acts 13:1-3)

An apostle desires to minister in places where others have not worked:

Yea, so have I strived to preach the gospel, not where Christ was named, lest I should build upon another man's foundation;

But as it is written, To whom He was not spoken of, they shall see: and they that have not heard shall understand. (Romans 15:20-21)

To preach the gospel in the regions beyond you, and not to boast in another man's line of things made ready to our hand.
(II Corinthians 10:16)

The apostle is willing to adapt to other cultures and lifestyles in order to win people for Christ:

For though I be free from all men, yet have I made myself servant unto all, that I might gain the more.

And unto the Jews I became as a Jew, that I might gain the Jews; to them that are under the law, as under the law, that I might gain them that are under the law;

To them that are without law, as without law, (being not without law to God, but under the law of Christ,) that I might gain them that are without law.

To the weak became I as weak, that I might gain the weak: I am made all things to all men, that I might by all means save some.

And this I do for the gospel's sake... (I Corinthians 9:19-23)

The apostle develops churches with trained leadership that can carry on without him:

And when they had preached the gospel to that city and had taught many, they returned again to Lystra, and to Iconium, and Antioch.

Confirming the souls of the disciples, and exhorting them to continue in the faith, and that we must through much tribulation enter into the kingdom of God.

And when they had ordained them elders in every church, and had prayed with fasting, they commended them to the Lord, on whom they believed. (Acts 14:21-23)

This verse reveals that follow up ministry and the raising up of qualified leadership for new churches are responsibilities of an apostle.

The seal, or evidence, of the apostolic gift is the spiritual result it brings in the lives of others. Paul wrote to the church at Corinth which he had organized:

...of the seal of mine apostleship are ye in the Lord. (I Corinthians 9:2b)

The ability to raise up communities of believers and organize them into a church body is the seal of the gift of apostleship.

The Bible warns of false apostles who are deceitful but can be recognized by their works:

For such are false apostles, deceitful workers, transforming themselves into the apostles of Christ.

And no marvel: for Satan himself is transformed into an angel of light.

Therefore it is no great thing if his ministers also be transformed as the ministers of righteousness; whose end shall be according their works. (II Corinthians 11:13-15)

FOR FURTHER STUDY:

The New Testament gives several examples of those who had the apostolic gift. Use these references for further study:

-Paul:	Galatians 1:1
-Andronicus and Junia:	Romans 16:7
-Apollos:	I Corinthians 4:6,9
-James:	Galatians 1:9
-Apostles of Jesus:	Gospels; book of Acts

PROPHETS

And God hath set some in the church, first apostles, secondarily prophets... (I Corinthians 12:28)

And He gave some apostles; and some, prophets... (Ephesians 4:11)

There are two prophetic gifts. One is the special gift of being a prophet. The other is the speaking gift of prophecy. In general, prophecy refers to speaking under the special inspiration of God. It is the special ability to receive and communicate an immediate message of God to His people through a divinely-anointed utterance. To this point, the definition applies to the special leadership gift of a prophet as well as the speaking gift of prophecy.

But a person is not a prophet just because he prophesies. Paul told the whole church to desire the gift of prophecy:

> **Follow after charity, and desire spiritual gifts, but rather that ye may prophesy. (I Corinthians 14:1)**
>
> **For ye may all prophesy one by one, that all may learn, and all may be comforted. (I Corinthians 14:31)**

But Paul indicated that not everyone was a prophet. He asked:

> **Are all prophets? (I Corinthians 12:29)**

The difference between a prophet and prophesying is apparent in the following passage:

> **And the next day we that were of Paul's company departed, and came unto Caesarea; and we entered into the house of Philip the evangelist, which was one of the seven; and abode with him.**
>
> **And the same man had four daughters, virgins, which did prophesy.**
>
> **And as we tarried there many days, there came down from Judaea a certain prophet, named Agabus. (Acts 21:8-11)**

Philip's daughters had the speaking gift of prophesy. But Agabus was a prophet who not only gave prophetic messages but held a leadership position in the church. God used him in a leadership role regarding Paul's ministry. Agabus gave Paul spiritual direction regarding what would happen in Jerusalem (Acts 21:11).

Those with the special gift of being a prophet do not just speak under the inspiration of God. They also hold an office of authority and leadership in the church. This is confirmed in Acts 13:1-4 where prophets and teachers were used in a leadership capacity to guide Barnabas and Saul into the special ministry to which God had called them.

In the Old Testament people went to prophets for guidance. The gift of Holy Spirit infilling was not yet given. The presence of God was shut up in the Holy of Holies. Because of the death and resurrection of Jesus Christ we now have access to the presence of God. The gift of the Holy Spirit has been given and, as you previously learned, one of His purposes is guidance:

> **For as many as are led by the Spirit of God, they are the sons of God. (Romans 8:14)**

It is no longer necessary to go to a prophet to receive spiritual guidance. This is one of the functions of the Holy Spirit in the life of the believer. Each believer should learn how to be led by God's Spirit. The New Testament gives no record of believers seeking guidance from prophets after the gift of the Holy Spirit was given.

But God still uses this gift to confirm guidance He has already given to a believer through the Holy Spirit. This is what happened in the case of Agabus and Paul. Paul already knew he was to go to Jerusalem. The prophecy of Agabus revealed what would happen to him there. It was not a prophecy of guidance telling Paul whether or not to go to Jerusalem.

The words spoken by a prophet under divine inspiration are called prophecies. To prophesy means to declare openly words from God that exhort, edify, and comfort:

> **But he that prophesieth speaketh unto men to edification, and exhortation, and comfort. (I Corinthians 14:3)**

Prophecy ministers not only to believers through edification but also to the unsaved. Prophecy can convict unbelievers and cause them to turn to the Lord:

> **But if all prophesy, and there come in one that believeth not, or one unlearned, he is convinced of all, he is judged of all:**
>
> **And thus are the secrets of his heart made manifest; and so falling down on his face he will worship God, and report that God is in you of a truth. (I Corinthians 14:24-25)**

One of the purposes of a prophet is to bring people to repentance:

> **Yet He sent prophets to them, to bring them again unto the Lord; and they testified against them; but they would not give ear. (II Chronicles 24:19)**

The Bible refers to prophecy as a great gift and more to be desired than the gift of tongues:

> **Follow after charity, and desire spiritual gifts, but rather that ye may prophesy.**

For he that speaketh in an unknown tongue speaketh not unto men, but unto God: for no man understandeth him; howbeit in the Spirit he speaketh mysteries.

But he that prophesieth speaketh unto men to edification and exhortation and comfort. (I Corinthians 14:1-3)

I would that ye all spake with tongues, but rather that ye prophesied; for greater is he that prophesieth than he that speaketh with tongues, except he interpret, that the church may receive edifying. (I Corinthians 14:5)

Wherefore brethren, covet to prophesy, and forbid not to speak with tongues. (I Corinthians 14:39)

The Holy Spirit is always in control of true prophecy and directs attention to Jesus Christ:

Now, concerning spiritual gifts, brethren, I would not have you ignorant.

Ye know that ye were Gentiles, carried away unto these dumb idols, even as ye were led.

Wherefore I give you to understand, that no man speaking by the Spirit of God calleth Jesus accursed; and that no man can say that Jesus is the Lord, but by the Holy Ghost. (I Corinthians 12:1-3)

Prophecy is never to replace the written Word of God. The Bible says prophecy will cease, but the Word of God abides forever:

...but whether there be prophecies, they shall fail... (I Corinthians 13:8)

But the word of the Lord endureth for ever. And this is the word which by the gospel is preached unto you. (I Peter 1:25)

The Bible warns of false prophets (Matthew 24:11,24; Mark 13:22). A person called "the false prophet" will be evident in events at the end of the world (Revelation 13:11-17; 16:13; 19:20; 20:10).

Because there are false prophets, God's word provides several ways to identify true prophecies. You can recognize them by:

1. DOCTRINAL ERROR:

Having then gifts differing according to the grace that is given to us, whether

prophecy, let us prophesy according to the proportion of faith. (Romans 12:6)

The phrase "in proportion to faith" means in right relation to the faith. The way to recognize true prophecies is by whether or not they agree with the basic doctrines of the Christian faith revealed in the Bible. For example, false prophets do not confess the deity of Jesus Christ:

Beloved, believe not every spirit, but try the spirits whether they are of God: because many false prophets are gone out into the world.

Hereby know ye the Spirit of God: Every spirit that confesseth that Jesus Christ is come in the flesh is of God:

And every spirit that confesseth not that Jesus Christ is come in the flesh is not of God: and this is the spirit of antichrist... (I John 4:1-3)

False prophets teach sexual immorality and permissiveness:

But there were false prophets also among the people, even as there shall be false teachers among you, who privily shall bring in damnable heresies, even denying the Lord that bought them, and bring upon themselves swift destruction.

And many shall follow their pernicious ways; by reason of whom the way of truth shall be evil spoken of.

And through covetousness shall they with feigned words make merchandise of you... (II Peter 2:1-3)

False prophets try to lead people away from obedience to God's Word (Deuteronomy 13:1-5). This type of prophecy is not in right relation to the Christian faith.

2. DECEIVING SIGNS:

False prophets deceive people with miraculous signs:

And many false prophets shall rise, and shall deceive many.

For there shall arise false Christs, and false prophets, and shall shew great signs and wonders; insomuch that, if it were possible, they shall deceive the very elect. (Matthew 24:11,24)

3. BAD FRUIT:

The evidence of spiritual fruit is the true test of any ministry:

> **Beware of false prophets, which come to you in sheep's clothing, but inwardly they are ravening wolves.**
>
> **Ye shall know them by their fruits... (Matthew 7:15-16)**

In Chapter Eleven you will study the fruit of the Holy Spirit. These are spiritual qualities which a true prophet will have.

4. FALSE CLAIMS:

Any prophet who claims to be divine or the same as Christ is false:

> **Then if any man shall say unto you, Lo, here is Christ, or there; believe it not.**
>
> **For there shall arise false christs, and false prophets, and shall shew great signs and wonders; insomuch that, if it were possible, they shall deceive the very elect. (Matthew 24:23-24)**

5. UNFULFILLED PROPHECIES:

The final test by which a true prophet can be identified is whether or not what he has prophesied comes to pass:

> **But the prophet, which shall presume to speak a word in my name, which I have not commanded him to speak, or that shall speak in the name of other gods, even that prophet shall die.**
>
> **And if thou say in thine heart, How shall we know the word which the Lord hath not spoken?**
>
> **When a prophet speaketh in the name of the Lord, if the thing follow not, nor come to pass, that is the thing which the Lord hath not spoken, but the prophet hath spoken it presumptuously; thou shalt not be afraid of him. (Deuteronomy 18:20-22)**

FOR FURTHER STUDY:

Prophecy can come from three different sources:

-The human spirit:	Jeremiah 23:16; Ezekiel 13:2,3
-Evil and lying spirits:	Isaiah 8:19-20; I Kings 22:22; Matthew 8:29; Acts 16:17
-The Holy Spirit:	II Samuel 23:2; Jeremiah 1:9; Acts 19:6; 21:11

This is why we must judge prophecies to determine whether or not they are from the Holy Spirit.

The Bible gives many examples of Old and New Testament prophets for you to study to increase your understanding of prophets and the gift of prophecy. As you study these references try to distinguish between those who had the special gift of being a prophet [leadership] from those who had just the gift of prophecy.

Old Testament Prophets:

Abraham:	Genesis 20:7
Moses:	Deuteronomy 34:9
Habakkuk:	Habakkuk 1:1
Isaiah:	II Kings 19:2
Micah:	Matthew 2:5-6
Hosea:	Matthew 21:15
Ephriam:	Hosea 9:8
Joel:	Acts 2:16
Jeremiah:	Jeremiah 1:5
Gad:	I Samuel 22:15
Zechariah:	Zechariah: 1:1
Ahijah:	I Kings 11:29
Samuel:	I Samuel 3:20
Jehu:	I Kings 16:7
Nathan:	II Samuel 7:2
Michaiah:	I Kings 22:7-8
Jonah:	II Kings 14:25
Iddo:	II Chronicles 13:22
Azzur:	Jeremiah 28:1
Ezekiel:	Ezekiel 2:1-5
Hananiah:	Jeremiah 28:17
Daniel:	Matthew 24:15
Balaam:	II Peter 2:15-16
Amos:	Acts 7:42-43
Shemh:	II Chronicles 12:5

Elisha:	I Kings 19:16
Elijah:	I Kings 18:22
Haggai:	Haggai 1:1
David:	Acts 2:29-30
Aaron:	Exodus 7:1
Azariah:	II Chronicles 15:8
Obed:	II Chronicles 15:8
Asaph:	Psalms 78:2

Old Testament Prophetessess (female):

Miriam:	Exodus 15:20
Deborah:	Judges 4:4
Huldah:	II Kings 22:14
Noadiah:	Nehemiah 6:14
Isaiah's Wife:	Isaiah 8:3

New Testament Prophets:

Jesus:	Matthew 21:11
John the Baptist:	Matthew 11:7-11
Agabus:	Acts 11:27-28; 21:10
Judas:	Acts 15:32
Silas:	Acts 15:32
Antioch Leaders:	Acts 13:1

New Testament Prophetesses (female):

Anna:	Luke 2:36
Philip's Daughters:	Acts 21:8-9

Study the guidelines for using prophecy when the church meets together: I Corinthians 14:29-31

EVANGELISTS

> **And He gave some apostles; and some prophets; and some, evangelists, and some pastors and teachers. (Ephesians 4:11)**

An evangelist has a special ability to share the Gospel with non-believers in a way that men and women respond and become responsible members of the Body of Christ. The meaning of the word "evangelist" is "one who brings good news."

The Word evangelist occurs three times in the New Testament. In Ephesians it is listed as one of the special gifts:

And He gave some...evangelists... (Ephesians 4:11)

Timothy is told to do the work of an evangelist:

But watch thou in all things, endure afflictions, do the work of an evangelist, make full proof of thy ministry. (II Timothy 4:5)

Although all believers are to "do the work of an evangelist" and share the Gospel with others, God gives some the special gift of being an evangelist. Philip was one who had the spiritual gift of being an evangelist:

And the next day we that were of Paul's company departed, and came unto Caesarea; and we entered in to the house of Philip the evangelist... (Acts 21:8)

Philip is actually the only person in the New Testament called an evangelist. His tendency towards this gift was evident from early in his experience with Christ. When Philip met Jesus the first thing he did was to share the news with Nathanael:

Philip findeth Nathanael, and saith unto him, We have found him, of whom Moses in the law and the prophets, did write, Jesus of Nazareth, the son of Joseph.

And Nathanael said unto him, Can there any good thing come out of Nazareth? Philip saith unto him, Come and see. (John 1:45-46)

Later Philip directed spiritually hungry Greeks to Jesus:

The same came therefore to Philip...and desired him, saying, Sir, we would see Jesus.

Philip cometh and telleth Andrew, and again, Andrew and Philip tell Jesus. (John 12:21-22)

Philip was chosen as a disciple (Matthew 10:3) and was in the upper room when the Holy Spirit came (Acts 1:13). Philip was ordained by man as a deacon in the church (Acts 6:1-6) but set by God as an evangelist (Ephesians 4:11-12).

FOR FURTHER STUDY:

Further study of the ministry of Philip will expand your knowledge of the special gift of being an evangelist:

-His message:	Acts 8:35
-Deliverance, miracles, healings:	Acts 8:5-8
-Baptized:	Acts 8:12,36-38
-Preached [the Kingdom of God]:	Acts 8:12
-House was set in order:	Acts 21:8-9
-Traveled to spread the Gospel:	Acts 8:4-5,26,40
-Ability to persuade groups:	Acts 8:6
-Stirred entire cities:	Acts 8:8
-Ministered to individuals:	Acts 8:27-38
-Led by God:	Acts 8:26,39
-Knowledge of the Word of God:	Acts 8:30-35
-Known by effectiveness of ministry and response of people:	Acts 8:5-6,8,12,35-39

PASTORS

> **And He gave some apostles; and some prophets; and some, evangelists, and some pastors and teachers. (Ephesians 4:11)**

This is the only place in the King James version of the New Testament where the word "pastor" is used. The Greek word "pastor" actually means shepherd. (The New Testament was originally written in Greek). Pastors are leaders who assume long-term personal responsibility for the spiritual welfare of a group of believers. Because the word means shepherd, pastors should follow the example set by Jesus Christ as a "pastor" or "shepherd" of people:

> **Now the God of peace, that brought again from the dead our Lord Jesus, that great shepherd of the sheep... (Hebrews 13:20)**

> **And when the chief Shepherd shall appear, ye shall receive a crown of glory that fadeth not away. (I Peter 5:4)**

Jesus also referred to Himself as the good shepherd and listed some of the functions of a shepherd in John 10:1-18.

The Bible mentions the office of a bishop (I Timothy 3). Many believe this is the same as a pastor because of the following verse spoken of Jesus:

> **For ye were as sheep going astray: but are now returned unto the Shepherd and Bishop of your souls. (I Peter 2:25)**

The spiritual requirements for bishops, elders, and deacons, which were positions of leadership in the early church, should certainly also be met by one who would lead these people as a pastor. Study these in I Timothy 3:1-13.

The responsibilities of a pastor are to spiritually feed and protect those under his ministry. This is to be done with a proper motive and not just for financial gain:

> **Take heed therefore unto yourselves, and to all the flock, over the which the Holy Ghost hath made you overseers, to feed the church of God, which He hath purchased with His own blood. (Acts 20:28)**
>
> **Feed the flock of God which is among you taking the oversight thereof, not for filthy lucre, but of a ready minds;**
>
> **Neither as being lords over God's heritage, but being ensamples to the flock.**
>
> **And when the chief shepherd shall appear, ye shall receive a crown of glory that fadeth not away. (I Peter 5:2-4)**

The word "pastor" is used in the Old Testament only in the book of Jeremiah. Here, God gives special warnings to pastors:

> **...the pastors also transgressed against me. (Jeremiah 2:8)**
>
> **For the pastors are become brutish, and have not sought the Lord; therefore they shall not prosper, and all their flocks shall be scattered. (Jeremiah 10:21)**
>
> **Many pastors have destroyed my vineyard, they have trodden my portion under foot, they have made my pleasant portion a desolate wilderness.**
>
> **They have made it desolate, and being desolate it mourneth unto me; the whole land is made desolate because no man layeth it to heart. (Jeremiah 12:10-11)**
>
> **Woe be unto the pastors that destroy and scatter the sheep of my pasture, saith the Lord.**
>
> **Therefore thus saith the Lord God of Israel against the pastors that feed my people; Ye have scattered my flock, and drive them away, and have not visited them: behold, I will visit upon you the evil of your doings, saith the Lord. (Jeremiah 23:1-2)**

FOR FURTHER STUDY:

Study the requirements for being a bishop or deacon in the church in I Timothy 3:1-13. These also apply for one who serves as a pastor. Study the characteristics of Jesus as the Good Shepherd given in John 10:1-18.

TEACHERS

> **And He gave some apostles; and some prophets; and some, evangelists, and some pastors and teachers. (Ephesians 4:11)**

Teachers are believers who have the special ability of communicating the Word of God effectively in such a way that others learn and apply what is taught. Teaching involves training, not just communicating information. The Bible records:

> **And He gave some...teachers... (Ephesians 4:11)**

> **And God hath set some in the church....thirdly, teachers...**
> **(I Corinthians 12:28)**

> **...Or he that teacheth on teaching... (Romans 12:7)**

Not all believers receive the special gift of teaching. Paul asked:

> **...are all teachers? (I Corinthians 12:29)**

His answer to this question was "no." God gives some the special gift of teaching.

The special gift of being a teacher differs from the speaking gift of teaching just as being a prophet differs from the speaking gift of prophecy. You will recall that Acts 13:1-4 showed teachers in a special leadership position [along with the prophets] in guiding the ministry of Paul and Barnabas. All believers do not have the special gift of teaching or the speaking gift of teaching. But all believers are to be involved in teaching the basic Gospel message:

> **For when for the time ye ought to be teachers, ye have need that one teach you again which be the first principles of the oracles of God...**
> **(Hebrews 5:12)**

All mature believers are to be involved in teaching the Gospel whether or not they have the special gift of teaching. (Because of this, Harvestime International Institute offers a separate course entitled *"Teaching Tactics"* to provide further instruction in this area).

The Bible warns of false teachers. These are people who claim to have the gift of teaching but do not teach the true Word of God:

> **But there were false prophets also among the people, even as there shall be false teachers among you, who privily shall bring in damnable heresies, even denying the Lord that bought them, and bring upon themselves swift destruction. (II Peter 2:1)**
>
> **For the time will come when they will not endure sound doctrine; but after their own lusts shall they heap to themselves teachers, having itching ears;**
>
> **And they shall turn away their ears from the truth, and shall be turned unto fables. (II Timothy 4:3-4)**
>
> **...thy teachers have transgressed against me...(Isaiah 43:27)**

II Peter chapter 2 and the book of Jude list some of the personal characteristics by which you can recognize false teachers.

It is possible to have a wrong motive for teaching as well as false doctrine:

> **Whose mouths must be stopped, who subvert whole houses, teaching things which they ought not for filthy lucre's sake. (Titus 1:11)**

Those who have been taught God's Word should teach faithful believers who will be able to teach others:

> **Let him that is taught in the word communicate unto him that teacheth in all good things. (Galatians 6:6)**
>
> **And the same thing that thou hast heard of me among many witnesses, the same commit thou to faithful men, who shall be able to teach others also. (II Timothy 2:2)**

This is the pattern of continuous teaching that, if followed, rapidly multiplies to spread the Gospel throughout the world.

A person with the spiritual gift of teaching does not teach man's wisdom:

> **Which things also we speak, not in the word which man's wisdom teacheth, but which the Holy Ghost teacheth; comparing spiritual things with spiritual. (I Corinthians 2:13)**

A teacher should have Godly understanding and wisdom. Paul warns against those who are...

> **...desiring to be teachers of the law; understanding neither what they say, nor whereof they affirm. (I Timothy 1:7)**

He stresses the importance of teaching with wisdom:

> **...Christ in you, the hope of glory:**
>
> **Whom we preach, warning every man, and teaching every man in all wisdom; that we may present every man perfect in Christ Jesus. (Colossians 1:27-28)**

Teachers must live what they teach:

> **Thou therefore which teachest another, teachest thou not thyself? thou that preachest a man should not steal, dost thou steal?**
>
> **Thou that sayest a man should not commit adultery, dost thou commit adultery? thou that abhorrest idols, dost thou commit sacrilege? (Romans 2:21-22)**

Teachers will be judged on the basis of what they have taught:

> **My brethren, be not many masters, knowing that we shall receive the greater condemnation. (James 3:1)**

FOR FURTHER STUDY:

Study the following examples of teachers in the New Testament. Who do you think might have had the special gift of being a teacher [a leadership position in the church]. Who might have had only the speaking gift of teaching?

-Appollos:	Acts 18:24-25
-Aquilla and Priscilla:	Acts 18:26
-Paul:	Acts 20:20-21,27; 21:28
-Unnamed:	Acts 13:1
-Peter:	Acts 5:28-29

Obtain the Harvestime International Institute course entitled *"Teaching Tactics."* It focuses on the tactics used by the greatest teacher, the Lord Jesus Christ.

LEADERSHIP WORKING TOGETHER

The five special gifts of leadership function together in the ministry of the church.

Apostles extend the Gospel message to various regions and raise up organized bodies of believers. God gives special miraculous signs and wonders to assist in this extension of the Gospel. The apostle provides special leadership to the churches he raises up.

Prophets also provide leadership in the church. One of their functions is to give special messages from God through the inspiration of the Holy Spirit.

Evangelists communicate the Gospel in such a manner that people respond to it and become believers. They may minister individually or in large groups, but their ministry always produces new believers. These believers then come under the care of apostles, prophets, pastors, and teachers of the church who guide their spiritual development. The example of Philip in Acts chapter 8 illustrates this. He brought the Samaritans to Christ, then turned them to the apostles for further teaching.

Pastors exercise long-term leadership and care for those who have believed through the message of the evangelist. They provide pastoral care to those who have become believers through the ministry of apostles. Their ministry is a picture of the loving care of a shepherd for his sheep.

Teachers provide instruction which goes beyond the presentation of the Gospel by the evangelist. They teach believers to be spiritually mature. They train faithful people who are capable of teaching others.

The main responsibility of those with special leadership gifts is to train other believers to discover and use their spiritual gifts (Ephesians 4:11-16). The following chart illustrates how the special gifts function together in the church:

GOD

GIVES

APOSTLES PROPHETS EVANGELISTS PASTORS TEACHERS

FOR

PERFECTING/EQUIPPING OF SAINTS

WHO WILL

MINISTER EDIFY

RESULTING IN

UNITY KNOWLEDGE PERFECTNESS

THAT THE BODY OF CHRIST MAY BE

NO MORE CHILDREN (false doctrine) GROW UP IN HIM (truth)

FINAL RESULT:

EFFECTIVE WORKING OF ALL PARTS OF THE BODY IN LOVE

SELF-TEST

1. Write the Key Verse from memory.

____

____

2. List the five special leadership gifts discussed in this chapter:

____

____

____

____

____

3. Why are these called "special gifts"?

____

____

4. Read each statement. If the statement is TRUE write T on the blank in front of it. If the statement is FALSE write F on the blank in front of it.

   a._____Everyone who prophesies does not necessarily have the special gift of being a prophet.

   b._____Everyone who teaches does not necessarily have the special gift of being a teacher.

   c._____Every believer should teach the Gospel to others, but this does not mean that all believers have the gift of teaching.

5. Look at the special gifts in list one. Read the definitions in list two. Write the number of the definition which describes the spiritual gift on the blank provided. The first one is done as an example for you.

List One	**List Two**
__2__Prophet	1. Sent with authority to act for another to develop new churches and oversee them.
_____Apostle	2. Speaks under special inspiration to communicate an immediate message of God to His people; also a leadership position.
_____Pastor	3. Shares the Gospel with nonbelievers in a way that they respond and become responsible members of the Body of Christ; "one who brings the good news."
_____Evangelist	4. Assumes long-term leadership for the spiritual welfare of believers; the word means shepherd.
_____Teacher	5. Communicates God's Word in such a way that others will learn and apply what is taught; also a leadership position.

6. What are the four major divisions of spiritual gifts being used for study purposes in this and the following chapters:

____

____

____

____

(Answers to tests are provided at the conclusion of the final chapter in this manual.)

FOR FURTHER STUDY

Suggestions for further study were given as each special gift was discussed in this chapter. This was done to permit you to complete your study of each gift before going on to study the next one. Believers with special gifts are leaders God sets in the church. But these are not the only church leadership positions mentioned in the Bible.

The offices of deacons and elders are mentioned in the New Testament. The position of bishop is also mentioned. Some churches consider a bishop the same as a pastor. Others consider it a separate office. These positions of leadership are not the same as the special gifts of leadership we have just studied. They are special offices established by the early church through the leading of the Lord.

The record of the early church was preserved by God as an example for us to follow in church structure. These offices should also function in the church today. The purpose of these offices is to assist those who have the special gifts of leadership discussed in this chapter, i.e., the apostles, prophets, evangelists, pastors, and teachers. Use the following outline to study these positions of leadership.

CHURCH OFFICES

Title	References	Duties
Bishop	I Timothy 3:1-7 Philippians 1:1 Titus 1:5-9 I Peter 5:2-3	Many consider a bishop to be the same as a pastor. these verses do indicate he is to have long term care over a group of believers.
Deacon	I Timothy 3:8-13 Philippians 1:1 Acts 6:1-7	These verses indicate deacons have a ministry of serving and helps.
Deaconesses	I Timothy 3:11 Romans 16:1-2	Deaconesses are not mentioned specifically in the Bible. Some churches have adopted this term for the wives of deacons or other women who minister in serving and helps.
Elders	Acts 20:17,28-32 Acts 14:23;15 Acts 16:4; 11:30 I Timothy 5:17 I Peter 5:1-4 Titus 1:5; James 5:14	These verses indicate elders provide leadership in the church and decisions, minister to the needs of believers and assist in the development and care of local bodies of believers.

Note: The word "elders" is first used in the Bible in Exodus 3:16 in reference to the leaders of Israel. There are many references to the elders of Israel throughout the Bible. These elders are different from the position of leadership known as an elder in the early church. All of the verses we have listed here refer to the elders in the church rather than the elders of Israel.

Observe that the elders function in leadership along with the special gifts of leadership God has set in the church. The elders are not to run the church independent of the special leaders of God, i.e., prophets, apostles, evangelists, pastors, teachers. God has set the special leaders in the church. Man chooses the elders.

QUALIFICATIONS

The Bible gives specific qualifications which are to be met by those filling these church offices:

BISHOPS AND ELDERS:

-Above reproach [Should have a good reputation and not be in violation of God's Word]: I Timothy 3:2; Titus 1:6,7

-Husband of one wife [If married, should have only one mate]: I Timothy 3:2; Titus 1:6

-Temperate [Moderate in all things]: Titus 1:8; I Timothy 3:2

-Self-controlled [Demonstrates control in all areas of life and conduct]: Titus 1:8

-Sober, vigilant [Prudent, sensible, wise and practical]: I Timothy 3:2; Titus 1:8

-Hospitable [Home is open to others]: I Timothy 3:2; Titus 1:8

-Able to teach [Has an ability communicate God's Word to others]: I Timothy 3:2; Titus 1:9

-Not addicted to wine: I Timothy 3:3; Titus 1:7

-Patient [The opposite of being quick tempered]: I Timothy 3:3

-Not self-willed [Not self-centered and always wanting their own way]: Titus 1:7

-Not a new convert [Must have maturity and experience as a believer]: I Timothy 3:6

-Loving what is good [Supporting all that is worthwhile to God and His purposes]: Titus 1:8

-Just [Fair in dealing with people]: Titus 1:8

-Stable in the Word: Titus 1:9

-Holy [Righteous, sanctified]: Titus 1:8

-Not fond of sordid gain [Not known for greed for financial gain. Free from the love of money]: Titus 1:7; I Timothy 3:3

-Manages his own household well [Must show leadership ability in his own family]: I Timothy 3:4-5

-Having children who believe [Must have children who have responded to the Lord and are not rebellious]: Titus 1:6

-Good reputation with those outside [Must have a good testimony among non-believers]: I Timothy 3:7

DEACONS:

-Dignity [Must be respected and demonstrate a serious mind and character]: I Timothy 3:8

-Not double tongued [Does not give conflicting reports]: I Timothy 3:8

-Not addicted to much wine: I Timothy 3:8

-Not fond of sordid gain [Not greedy for financial gain]: I Timothy 3:8

-Settled in his commitment to the faith: I Timothy 3:9

-Tested [A person who has undergone spiritual trials and temptations and proven faithful]: I Timothy 3:10

-Beyond reproach [The absence of any charge of violation in conduct]: I Timothy 3:10

-Husband of one wife [If married should have one mate]: I Timothy 3:12

-Good managers of children and household [Must demonstrate leadership in family life]: I Timothy 3:12

-Proven [Not a new convert, but proven as a believer]: I Timothy 3:10

DEACONESS:

-Women: I Timothy 3:11

-Dignified [Respected and demonstrate a serious mind and character]: I Timothy 3:11

-Not malicious gossips [Does not talk about others in a slanderous way]: I Timothy 3:11

-Temperate [Moderate in all things]: I Timothy 3:11

-Faithful in all things [Trustworthy and dependable in every area of life]: I Timothy 3:11

-Helper of many [Must minister to others and help meet their needs]: Romans 16:2

CHURCH STRUCTURE

The Biblical structure of the church is shown in the following diagram:

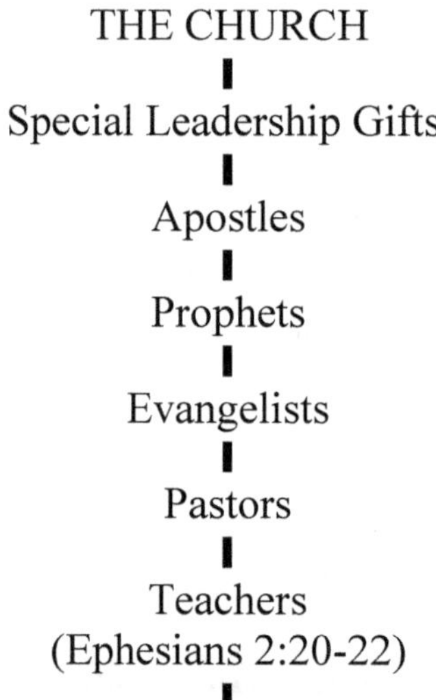

(assisted by special offices of bishops, deacons, elders, and each member of the body using their spiritual gift in the church in the place God has set them)

The Foundation Laid By Apostles and Prophets
Ephesians 2:20

BUILT UPON THE ROCK-JESUS CHRIST
Matthew 16:18 I Corinthians 3:11 Ephesians 2:20THE CHURCH

CHAPTER SEVEN

SPEAKING GIFTS OF THE HOLY SPIRIT

OBJECTIVES:

Upon completion of this chapter you will be able to:

- Identify the five speaking gifts.
- Define the speaking gifts.
- Distinguish between the word of wisdom and the word of knowledge.

KEY VERSE:

But now hath God set the members every one of them in the body, as it hath pleased Him. (I Corinthians 12:18)

INTRODUCTION

Five gifts have been given the title of "speaking gifts" because they all involve speaking aloud. The five speaking gifts are:

-Prophecy	-Exhortation	-Word of Knowledge
-Teaching	-Word of Wisdom	

The first two speaking gifts, prophecy and teaching, are similar to two of the special gifts. But the speaking gifts of prophecy and teaching are not the same as the special leadership gifts of being a prophet or a teacher.

PROPHECY

For to one is given by the Spirit...prophecy. (I Corinthians 12:10)

A person with the gift of prophecy speaks by the special inspiration of God to communicate an immediate message to His people. Prophecy was discussed in detail in the section on the special gift of being a prophet. Everything said there about prophecy given by a prophet also applies to the gift of prophecy. But the speaking gift of prophecy alone does not mean you have the special gift of being a prophet. As you previously learned, God has set prophets [who also have the gift of prophecy] in special leadership positions in the church.

Although they prophesy like prophets, people with the gift of prophecy do not have the special leadership position of a prophet. They simply deliver special messages under the inspiration of the Holy Spirit.

TEACHING

> **Having then gifts differing according to the grace that is given to us...let us wait on our ministering: or he that teacheth, on teaching...**
> **(Romans 12:6-7)**

The subject of teaching was covered in the section on the special gift of teaching. Everything discussed applies also to the gift of teaching with the exception of the leadership position.

As in the example of prophets and prophecy, the speaking gift of teaching does not mean a person has the special gift of being a teacher. God sets teachers [who also have the gift of teaching] in special leadership positions in the church.

EXHORTATION

> **Having then gifts differing according to the grace that is given to us...he that exhorteth on exhortation... (Romans 12:6,8)**

The gift of exhortation is the ability to draw close to individuals in time of need, counseling them correctly with the Word of God. To "exhort" literally means to call a person aside, to advise, recommend, admonish, encourage, or comfort.

Exhortation is the ability to give wise spiritual counsel. People with this gift minister words of comfort, consolation, and encouragement in such a way that others are helped. A modern term for this gift would be "the gift of counseling."

Exhortation was part of the apostle's follow up plan for the churches:

> **And when they had preached the gospel to that city and had taught many, they returned again to Lystra, and to Iconium, and Antioch,**
>
> **Confirming the souls of the disciples, and exhorting them to continue in the faith.... (Acts 14:21-22)**

The Bible teaches how exhortation is to be done:

AS A FATHER WOULD HIS OWN CHILDREN:

> **As ye know how we exhorted and comforted and charged every one of you, as a father doth his children. (I Thessalonians 2:11)**

BY GIVING INSTRUCTION WITH PATIENCE:

> **Preach the word; be instant in season, out of season: reprove, rebuke, exhort with all longsuffering and doctrine. (II Timothy 4:2)**

ON THE BASIS OF SOUND BIBLICAL DOCTRINE:

> **Holding fast the faithful word as he hath been taught that he may be able by sound doctrine both to exhort and convince the gainsayers. (Titus 1:9)**

WITH ALL AUTHORITY:

> **These thing speak, and exhort, and rebuke with all authority... (Titus 2:15)**

MORE FREQUENTLY AS THE END OF TIME APPROACHES:

> **...but exhorting one another: and so much the more, as ye see the day approaching. (Hebrews 10:25)**

FOR FURTHER STUDY:

The Bible gives several examples of people who had the gift of exhortation and counseled others. Study these for further understanding of this gift:

-Barnabas:	Acts 11:22-24
-Judas and Silas:	Acts 15:32
-Paul:	Acts 14:22, II Corinthians 9:5, I Thessalonians 4:1
-Jude:	Jude 3

In what attitude should a person exhort another? See I Thessalonians 2:11 and 5:14.

____

When exhorted, what things were people encouraged to do?

I Peter 5:1-2 ______________________________

II Timothy 4:1-4 ______________________________

I Thessalonians 2:11-12 ______________________________

II Thessalonians 3:12 ______________________________

Study the following verses and complete the chart:

	Who	**Encouraged Whom**
Acts 14:21-22	___________	___________
Acts 16:40	___________	___________
Acts 20:1	___________	___________
II Corinthians 1:3-7	___________	___________

WORD OF WISDOM

For to one is given by the Spirit the word of wisdom... (I Corinthians 12:8)

The word of wisdom is the ability to receive insight as to how knowledge may be applied to specific needs. Given the facts in any situation, a person with this gift knows how to apply the facts to bring a wise solution.

The word of wisdom is a divine insight into people and situations that is not obvious to the average person. This God-given wisdom is combined with an understanding of what to do and how to do it. This gift is not called "the gift of wisdom" because it does not give one the total wisdom of God. It is a word of wisdom, just a portion of God's infinite wisdom.

The gift of the word of wisdom does not come through education. The source of such wisdom is God:

> **...to the acknowledgement of the mystery of God, and of the Father, and of Christ;**

In whom are hid all the treasures of wisdom and knowledge. (Colossians 2:2-3)

Jesus Christ was called the "wisdom of God":

But unto them which are called, both Jews and Greeks, Christ the power of God, and the wisdom of God.

But of Him are ye in Christ Jesus, who of God is made unto us wisdom, and righteousness, and sanctification, and redemption. (I Corinthians 1:24,30)

Godly wisdom is not the same as the wisdom of the world:

But if ye have bitter envying and strife in your hearts, glory not, and lie not against the truth.

This wisdom descendeth not from above, but is earthly, sensual, devilish.

For where envying and strife is, there is confusion and every evil work.

But the wisdom that is from above is first pure, then peaceable, gentle, and easy to be entreated, full of mercy and good fruits, without partiality, and without hypocrisy. (James 3:14-17)

If you do not have the gift of the word of wisdom you can still develop spiritual wisdom. You can receive it by studying the Word of God:

And that from a child thou hast known the holy Scriptures which are able to make thee wise unto salvation through faith which is in Christ Jesus. (II Timothy 3:15)

You can ask God for wisdom:

If any of you lack wisdom, let him ask of God, that giveth to all men liberally and upbraideth not; and it shall be given him. (James 1:5)

Wisdom is given to those who live a godly life:

For the Lord giveth wisdom; out of His mouth cometh knowledge and understanding.

He layeth up sound wisdom for the righteous; He is a buckler to them that walk uprightly. (Proverbs 2:6-7)

But remember, this spiritual wisdom available to all believers is not the same as the gift of the word of wisdom. The word of wisdom is a special ability given by God through the Holy Spirit.

FOR FURTHER STUDY:

Study the references made by Paul to wisdom: I Corinthians 2:1-13. What are the differences between the two wisdoms of which he writes? The word of wisdom was operative in his life. See II Peter 3:15-16; I Corinthians 2:4-8.

Wisdom was evident in the ministry of Stephen: Acts 6:3,10

King Solomon was the best example of wisdom in the Old Testament: I Kings 3:5-28

Study the book of Proverbs. It was written by King Solomon and is the practical application of spiritual wisdom.

Study James 3:17. List the characteristics of godly wisdom.

Study these examples of the word of wisdom in operation:

-Luke 2:40-52; 21:15
-Acts 5:26-33
 (observe wisdom in the statement "we ought to obey God rather than men").
-Deuteronomy 34:9
-Exodus 36:1-2

WORD OF KNOWLEDGE

For to one is given by the Spirit the word of wisdom; to another the word of knowledge by the same Spirit...(I Corinthians 12:8)

The word of knowledge is the ability to understand things which others do not know and cannot comprehend and to share this knowledge with them under the inspiration of the Spirit. Like the word of wisdom, it is not called "the gift of knowledge." It is the gift of the "word of knowledge." It is not the total knowledge of God, but only a portion of His knowledge.

The source of this spiritual knowledge is God:

In whom are hid all the treasures of wisdom and knowledge. (Colossians 2:3)

For what man knoweth the things of a man, save the spirit of man which is in him? Even so the things of God knoweth no man, but the Spirit of God.

Now we have received, not the spirit of the world, but the Spirit which is of God; that we might know the things that are freely given to us of God.

Which things also we speak, not in the words which man's wisdom teacheth, but which the Holy Ghost teacheth; comparing spiritual things with spiritual.

But the natural man receiveth not the things of the Spirit of God; for they are foolishness unto him; neither can he know them because they are spiritually discerned. (I Corinthians 2:11-14)

The gift of the word of knowledge is revelatory knowledge. This means it is knowledge revealed by God. It is not knowledge obtained through education or study.

When Jesus asked Peter a spiritual question and he answered with a word of knowledge, Jesus said:

Blessed art thou, Simon Barjona, for flesh and blood hath not revealed it unto thee, but my Father which is in Heaven. (Matthew 16:17)

The gift of the word of knowledge should be used in humility because you are not the source of the knowledge. God is the source:

...Knowledge puffeth up, but charity edifieth.

And if any man think that he knoweth any thing, he knoweth nothing yet as he ought to know. (I Corinthians 8:1-2)

FOR FURTHER STUDY:

New Testament examples of the word of knowledge for further study:

-Jesus:	John 1:48; 4:17-18; 11:14
-Simon:	Luke 2:25-35
-Ananias and Sapphira:	Acts 5:1-11
-Paul:	Acts 27:13-44
-Peter:	Acts 5:1-10; 8:23; 10:19
-Ananias:	Acts 9:1-18

Observe in this passage that Ananias:

-Knew where Paul was:	Verse 11
-Knew he was praying:	Verse 11
-Knew he had seen a vision:	Verse 12
-Knew he was a chosen vessel:	Verse 15
-Knew he would suffer:	Verse 16
-Knew he would be a witness:	Verse 15

SELF-TEST

1. Write the Key Verse from memory

____

2. What are the five speaking gifts?

 ____________ ____________ ____________ ___________ ____________

3. Read the list of speaking gifts in list one. Read the definitions in list two. Write the number of the definition which describes the gift on the blank provided.

List One	**List Two**
_____Exhortation	1. Speaks by special inspiration of God an immediate message to His people.
_____Prophecy	2. Words of counsel, comfort.
_____Word of Wisdom	3. Ability to train others in God's Word.
_____Teaching	4. Insight as to how knowledge may be applied to specific needs.
_____Word of Knowledge	5. Ability to understand things others cannot and to share under the inspiration of the Spirit.

4. Circle the correct answer to complete this sentence: Believers give a word of wisdom or knowledge by...

   a. Repeating what they have read.
   b. Trying to think of something God might want them to say.
   c. The Holy Spirit giving them a word to speak.

5. Is this statement True or False? The gifts of the word of wisdom and the word of knowledge are the same. The statement is_____________

(Answers to tests are provided at the conclusion of the final chapter in this manual.)

"For Further Study" for this lesson were given as each speaking gift was discussed in this chapter. This was done to permit you to complete your study of each gift before going on to the next one.

CHAPTER EIGHT

SERVING GIFTS OF THE HOLY SPIRIT

OBJECTIVES:

Upon completion of this chapter you will be able to:

- Identify the nine serving gifts of the Holy Spirit.
- Explain the difference between the gift of serving and the gift of helps.
- Explain the difference between the gift of administration and the gift of leadership.
- Distinguish between the gift of faith and the fruit of faith.

KEY VERSE:

> **And whosoever of you will be the chiefest, shall be servant of all.**
> **(Mark 10:44)**

INTRODUCTION

There are nine spiritual gifts which we will call the "serving gifts." These gifts are not special offices such as those of apostle, prophet, evangelist, pastor or teacher. They are not speaking gifts where one stands before the church body to minister the Word of God. Neither are they sign gifts (which you will study in the next chapter) which are given to confirm the truth of the Gospel.

These nine gifts "serve" the church by providing structure, organization, and support in both spiritual and practical areas. The nine serving gifts are:

-Discerning of spirits	-Helps
-Leadership	-Serving
-Administration	-Mercy
-Faith	-Hospitality
-Giving	

DISCERNING OF SPIRITS

> **But the manifestation of the Spirit is given to every man to profit withal.**
>
> **For to one is given by the Spirit...discerning of spirits...**
> **(I Corinthians 12:7-10)**

Discerning of spirits is the ability to evaluate people, doctrines, and situations as to whether they are of God or of Satan. In no way should discerning of spirits be confused with a critical spirit. The gift is a spiritual gift. Spiritual things are not discerned with the natural mind:

> **But the natural man receiveth not the things of the Spirit of God: for they are foolishness unto him; neither can he know them, because they are spiritually discerned. (I Corinthians 2:15)**

This gift is limited to the discerning of spirits. It is not just discerning in general. This gift serves the church by identifying people who would split the fellowship with wrong motives, doctrines, and attitudes.

Discerning of spirits is an important gift because the enemies against which we fight are not visible to the human eye. They are recognized only through spiritual discernment:

> **For we wrestle not against flesh and blood, but against principalities, against powers, against the rulers of the darkness of this world, against spiritual wickedness in high places. (Ephesians 6:12)**

One of the strategies used by Satan is deception. This is why discernment is so important:

> **And no marvel; for Satan himself is transformed into an angel of light.**
>
> **Therefore it is no great thing if his ministers also be transformed as the ministers of righteousness; whose end shall be according to their works.**
> **(II Corinthians 11:14-15)**

As we near the return of the Lord Jesus, these spirits of deception will increase:

> **Now the Spirit speaketh expressly, that in the latter times some shall depart from the faith, giving heed to seducing spirits, and doctrines of devils.**
> **(I Timothy 4:1)**

The Apostle Peter warned:

But there were false prophets also among the people, even as there shall be false teachers among you, who privily shall bring in damnable heresies, even denying the Lord that bought them, and bring upon themselves swift destruction.

And many shall follow their pernicious ways; by reason of whom the way of truth shall be evil spoken of. (II Peter 2:1-2)

If you do not have the gift of discerning of spirits you are not left defenseless. God has given a way to test the spirits. This test is valid whether or not you have the gift of discernment:

Beloved, believe not every spirit, but try the spirits whether they are of God: because many false prophets are gone out into the world.

Hereby know ye the Spirit of God: Every spirit that confesseth that Jesus Christ is come in the flesh is of God;

And every spirit that confesseth not that Jesus Christ is come in the flesh is not of God: and this is the spirit of antichrist, whereof ye have heard that it should come; and even now already is it in the world. (I John 4:1-3)

You can learn to use your spiritual senses to discern between good and evil.
These spiritual senses are developed by study of God's Word:

For every one that useth milk is unskillful in the word of righteousness; for he is a babe.

But strong meat belongeth to them that are of full age, even those who by reason of use have their senses exercised to discern both good and evil. (Hebrews 5:13-14)

FOR FURTHER STUDY:

The following references are examples of use of the gift of discerning of spirits:

-Jesus: Matthew 16:21-23; John 1:47; Luke 9:55
-Paul: Acts 13:6-12; 16:16-18
-Peter: Acts 5:1-11; 8:18-24

(In Acts 8:18-24, what is one intended result of the use of the gift of discerning of spirits?)

LEADERSHIP

> **Having then gifts differing according to the grace that is given to us...he that ruleth, with diligence... (Romans 12:6,8)**

The spiritual gift of leadership is the ability to set goals in accord with God's purpose and to communicate these goals to others. A person with this gift motivates and leads others to accomplish these goals for the glory of God.

Leadership is mentioned in Romans 12 and the qualification for this gift is that one leads [rules] with diligence. Diligence means to show constant care and effort to accomplish what is undertaken. It means to be industrious, attentive, and to persevere.

A person with the gift of leadership should lead his own family well:

> **For if a man know not how to rule his own house, how shall he take care of the church of God? (I Timothy 3:5)**

This is true for one with the gift of administration as well.

Believers should show respect for those who are leaders in the church:

> **And we beseech you, brethren, to know them which labour among you, and are over you in the Lord, and admonish you;**
>
> **And to esteem them very highly in love for their work's sake... (I Thessalonians 5:12-13)**

We are told to...

> **Obey them that have the rule over you, and submit yourselves: for they watch for your souls, as they that must give account, that they may do it with joy, and not with grief: for that is unprofitable for you. (Hebrews 13:17)**

FOR FURTHER STUDY:

Three of the greatest leaders were Moses, Joshua, and David. The story of Moses is found in the books of Exodus through Deuteronomy. Joshua's story is contained in the book of Joshua. You can read about David in the books of I and II Samuel.

Other great leaders were:

-Nehemiah:	Book of Nehemiah
-Ezra:	Ezra and Nehemiah
-Peter:	Book of Acts

ADMINISTRATION

And God hath set some in the church, first apostles, secondarily prophets, thirdly teachers, after that miracles, then gifts of healings, helps, governments, diversities of tongues. (I Corinthians 12:28)

The gift of administration is actually called "governments" in the Bible. A person with the gift of administration has the ability to give direction, organize, and make decisions on behalf of others. The meaning of the word administration is similar to the word used for a pilot steering a ship. A similar word is used for both in the Bible:

The inhabitants of Zidon and Arvad were they mariners; thy wise men, O Tyrus, that were in thee, were thy pilots. (Ezekiel 27:8)

A person with this gift is responsible for direction and decision making. Like the pilot of a ship he may not be the owner of the ship, but he has been entrusted with the responsibility of directing it on its voyage.

The gifts of leadership and administration both involve organizational skills which result in the accomplishing of spiritual goals. Often a believer will have both the gifts of leadership and administration. If a person has the gift of administration but does not have the gift of leadership, he will need someone with that gift to work with him.

A person with the gift of administration has the ability to direct, organize, and make decisions. But without the gift of leadership he does not have the ability to motivate and actually work with people to achieve goals.

Pastors and teachers often also have the spiritual gift of leadership. They are able to motivate people to accomplish spiritual goals. But many of them do not have the gift of administration. Although they motivate, they fail to organize in such a way that the goals can be achieved.

The relationship of Titus and Paul illustrates how the gift of administration functions. Among other gifts, Paul had the special leadership gift of being an apostle. He raised up a church in Crete, then Titus organized and directed it:

To Titus, mine own son...For this cause left I thee in Crete, that thou shouldest set in order the things that are wanting, and ordain elders in every city, as I had appointed thee. (Titus 1:5)

Paul had appointed Titus as administrator over the churches in Crete. Paul was still the authority in the churches. Titus was administrator carrying out his instructions. According to this passage, one of the functions of administration is to train other believers for leadership positions in the church.

FOR FURTHER STUDY:

Study the problem described in Acts 6:1-7. What was the problem? Who used the gift of leadership? Who might have had the gift of administration?

Read Luke 14:28-30. Observe the value of planning and organization. This is part of good administration.

Study the life of Joseph in Genesis 37 through 50. Joseph had a gift of administration. He organized and directed Egypt for Pharaoh. See also Acts 7:9-10.

FAITH

But the manifestation of the Spirit is given to every man to profit withal.

For to one is given by the Spirit...faith...(I Corinthians 12:7-9)

A person with the gift of faith has a special ability to believe with supernatural confidence and trust God in difficult circumstances. It is special faith to meet a special need. He knows God is going to do the impossible. He exercises this faith even when other believers around him do not believe. The Bible defines faith as:

...the substance of things hoped for, the evidence of thing not seen. (Hebrews 11:1)

The Amplified Bible adds to this definition:

Now faith is the assurance, the confirmation, the title deed of the things we hope for, being proof of things we do not see, and the conviction of their reality. Faith is the perceiving as real what is not revealed to the senses. (Hebrews 11:1, The Amplified Bible)

Faith gives assurance that the things promised in the future are true and that unseen things are real.

There are different kinds of faith. There is natural faith which is a trust in things that have proven stable. The Bible speaks of sanctifying faith (Galatians 2:20), defensive faith (Ephesians 6:16), and saving faith (Romans 5:1).

The Bible reveals there are various levels of faith. Jesus spoke of people who did not use their faith as being faithless (Matthew 17:17). He spoke of those with little faith (Matthew 6:30; 8:26: 14:31; Luke 12:28) and of those with great faith (Matthew 8:10; 15:28; Luke 7:9).

The Bible teaches that each person has a certain amount of faith given to him as a gift of God (Romans 12:3b). It also teaches that we are saved through faith (Ephesians 2:8). But the gift of faith is an unusual ability to believe God in every area of life. This faith knows no impossibilities. It puts no limits on what God can do.

> **For those who do not have the gift of faith the Bible tells how to increase faith:**
>
> **So then faith cometh by hearing, and hearing by the Word of God. (Romans 10:17)**

Faith is listed in Galatians 5:22 as a fruit of the Holy Spirit as well as a gift. Faith as a spiritual gift refers to power. As a fruit it refers to character. Faith as a gift is an act. It is the ability to act in faith in the face of impossibilities. Faith as a fruit is an attitude. It is developed through spiritual growth just as fruit in the natural world develops through growth processes.

FOR FURTHER STUDY:

Study Hebrews 11. This chapter gives many examples of those who had great faith. Make a list of the things these people accomplished by their faith.

-Abraham was called a man of faith:	Romans 4:16-21; Hebrews 11:18-19
-Stephen had the gift of faith:	Acts 6:5-8
-Barnabas possibly had it:	Acts 11:22-24
-Paul demonstrated great faith:	Acts 27.
-Faith emphasizes the impossible:	I Corinthians 13:2

GIVING

> **Having then gifts differing according to the grace that is given to us...he that giveth let him do it with simplicity... (Romans 12:6,8)**

A person with the gift of giving has a special ability to give material goods and financial resources to the work of the Lord. He does it with joy and eagerness. The gift of giving also includes the giving of time, strength, and talents to the work of the Lord. The one requirement for a person with the gift of giving is that it is done with simplicity. The word simplicity as used here means liberally.

All Christians are to give to the work of the Lord:

> **Every man according as he purposeth in his heart, so let him give, not grudgingly, or of necessity: for God loveth a cheerful giver. (II Corinthians 9:7)**

All believers are to give tithe from their income. The tithe is 10% of all that is earned. If believers do not give tithes and offerings, it is the same as robbing God:

> **Will a man rob God? Yet ye have robbed me. But ye say, Wherein have we robbed thee? In tithes and offerings. (Malachi 3:8)**

God has promised special blessings to those who tithe their income:

> **Bring ye all the tithes into the storehouse, that there may be meat in mine house, and prove me now herewith, saith the Lord of hosts, if I will not open you the windows of heaven, and pour you out a blessing, that there shall not be room enough to receive it.**
>
> **And I will rebuke the devourer for your sakes, and he shall not destroy the fruits of your ground; neither shall your vine cast her fruit before the time in the field, saith the Lord of hosts.**
>
> **And all nations shall call you blessed; for ye shall be a delightsome land, saith the Lord of hosts. (Malachi 3:10-12)**

According to this passage, those who give are promised:

1. Unnamed blessings from God, so great they cannot contain them. Verse 10
2. Blessings on the work which provides their income. Verse 11
3. They will be a blessing to the nations of the world. Verse 12
4. Their own land [nation] will be blessed. Verse 12

God blesses you financially upon the basis of how you give. He provides in order that you will have funds to give to the work of the Lord:

> **But this I say, he which soweth sparingly shall reap also sparingly; and he which soweth bountifully shall reap also bountifully...**

And God is able to make all grace abound toward you; that ye, always having all sufficiency in all things, may abound to every good work. (II Corinthians 9:6,8)

Jesus also promised:

Give, and it shall be given unto you; good measure, pressed down, and shaken together, and running over, shall men give into your bosom. For with the same measure that ye mete withal it shall be measured to you again. (Luke 6:38)

The way you are to acquire the money or goods to give is described in Ephesians:

Let him that stole steal no more; but rather let him labour, working with his hands, the thing which is good, that he may have to give to him that needeth. (Ephesians 4:28)

Paul commented regarding the giving of the Philippian believers:

...the things which were sent from you, an odour of a sweet smell, a sacrifice acceptable, well pleasing to God. (Philippians 4:18)

He indicated because their gifts were a sacrifice they had pleased God. Then he told these giving believers:

But my God shall supply all your need according to His riches in glory by Christ Jesus. (Philippians 4:19)

This promise was made to those who had given to the work of the Lord. But remember: Although all believers are to give and are blessed of God for doing so, a person with the gift of giving has an unusual ability to give joyfully to the Lord; a special spiritual motivation to give.

FOR FURTHER STUDY:

The following are Biblical examples of people who had an unusual ability to give to the Lord. It is possible they had the spiritual gift of giving:

-Widow:	Mark 12:41-44; Luke 21:1-4
-Mary:	John 12:3-8
-Galatian church:	Galatians 4:15
-Philippian church:	Philippians 4:10-18
-Macedonian churches:	II Corinthians 8:1-7

From what motivations must giving come? See Matthew 6:3; Ephesians 4:28; I Corinthians 13:3.

HELPS

> **And God hath set some in the church, first apostles, secondarily prophets, thirdly teachers, after that miracles, then gifts of healings, helps, governments, diversities of tongues. (I Corinthians 12:28)**

A person with the gift of helps has the ability to assist others in the work of the Lord enabling them to increase the effectiveness of their own spiritual gifts. From custodian to musicians, anything assisting in the operation of a church or a ministry can be considered a gift of helps. When Paul sent a woman named Phoebe to Rome, he asked believers there to assist her with the gift of helps:

> **I commend unto you Phoebe, our sister, which is a servant of the church which is at Cenchrea:**
>
> **That ye receive her in the Lord, as becometh saints, and that ye assist her in whatsoever business she hath need of you; for she hath been a succourer of many, and of myself also. (Romans 16:1-2)**

Priscilla and Aquila apparently served Paul with the gift of helps, for he wrote:

> **Greet Priscilla and Aquila, my helpers in Christ Jesus... (Romans 16:3)**

The gift of helps is any work which supports or assists someone else. It is like serving as an assistant.

FOR FURTHER STUDY:

-Tabitha [Dorcas] had the gift of helps: Acts 9:36
-Women helped Jesus in His ministry: Mark 15:40-41
-The help given could be in the area of organizational responsibilities: Exodus 18:22; Numbers 11:17
-The ministry of helps can assist those who are weak: Acts 20:35

SERVING

> **Having then gifts differing according to the grace that is given to us...or ministry, let us wait on our ministering... (Romans 12:6-7)**

The word "ministering" in this passage means serving. The gift of serving is an ability to perform practical tasks related to the work of the Lord. A person who serves helps others accomplish spiritual goals by freeing them from routine but necessary duties.

The Amplified Bible translates this passage...

> **...he whose gift is practical service, let him give himself to serving... (Romans 12:7)**

Serving differs from helps in that it relieves someone of certain duties. One who serves assumes the responsibility for certain tasks to free another to exercise their spiritual gift.

A person with the gift of helps assists someone in the performing of their ministry. For example, musicians in the church help the pastor accomplish spiritual goals during a church service. They do not relieve him of the responsibility of the service, but use their gift to help him accomplish spiritual objectives.

On the other hand, a person with the gift of serving might totally relieve a pastor from involvement in the distribution of food to those in need within the church body. An example of this is found in the early church where certain believers "served" tables to free the apostles for more important spiritual tasks:

> **And in those days when the number of the disciples was multiplied, there arose a murmuring of the Grecians against the Hebrews, because their widows were neglected in the daily ministration.**
>
> **Then the twelve called the multitude of the disciples unto them, and said, It is not reason that we should leave the word of God and serve tables.**
>
> **Wherefore, brethren, look ye out among you seven men of honest report, full of the Holy Ghost, and wisdom, whom we may appoint over this business.**
>
> **But we will give ourselves continually to prayer, and to the ministry of the word. (Acts 6:1-4)**

Observe the qualifications for those who were to serve. They were to be honest and full of the Holy Ghost and wisdom. Paul spoke of those who ministered or served him:

> **The Lord give mercy unto the house of Onesiphorus for he oft refreshed me, and was not ashamed of my chain:**
>
> **But when he was in Rome, he sought me out very diligently, and found me.**
>
> **The Lord grant unto him that he may find mercy of the Lord in that day: and in how many things he ministered unto me at Ephesus, thou knowest very well. (II Timothy 1:16-18)**

The gift of serving involves bearing the burden of others:

> **Bear ye one another's burdens, and so fulfill the law of Christ. (Galatians 6:2)**

The attitude of one who serves was described by Jesus:

> **And He said unto them, The kings of the Gentiles exercise lordship over them; and they that exercise authority upon them are called benefactors.**
>
> **But ye shall not be so: but he that is greatest among you, let him be as the younger, and he that is chief, as he that doth serve.**
>
> **For whether is greater, he that sitteth at meat, or he that serveth? Is not he that sitteth at meat? But I am among you as he that serveth. (Luke 22:25-27)**

FOR FURTHER STUDY:

Examples of serving:

-Angels:	Hebrews 1:14; 4:11; Mark 1:13
-Serving or waiting at meals:	John 2:5,9; Luke 10:40

MERCY

> **Having then gifts differing according to the grace that is given to us...he that showeth mercy, with cheerfulness. (Romans 12:6,8)**

"Mercy" means compassion. This means you are able to feel with and for another. A person with the gift of mercy has special compassion on those suffering and an ability to help them.

The gift of mercy involves an attitude as well as an action. This is shown in the story of the Good Samaritan recorded in Luke 10:30-37. The Samaritan not only had compassion on the victim of the robbers, but also took action to help him.

A requirement is that this gift should be ministered with cheerfulness. The word "cheerfulness" refers to a joyful readiness to do anything possible immediately to relieve suffering.

Compare the compassion of the disciples with that of Jesus as illustrated in the following events:

Reference	Jesus	Disciples
Matthew 15:23-28 Syrophoenician woman	Healed daughter	Send away
Mark 8:1-9 Multitudes	Fed them	Send away
Matthew 20:31-34 Blind men	Healed them	Tried to make them be quiet
Mark 10:48-49 Blind Bartemaus	Healed him	Tried to make him be quiet

FOR FURTHER STUDY:

Study these illustrations of the gift of mercy:

-Jesus, in connection with healing: Matthew 9:27-30; 15:21-28; 17:14-18; 20:30-34; Mark 10:46-52; Luke 17:1-14
-The Good Samaritan: Luke 10:30-37
-Dorcus: Acts 9:36-42

HOSPITALITY

Use hospitality one to another without grudging.

As every man hath received the gift, even so minister the same one to another, as good stewards of the manifold grace of God. (I Peter 4:9-10)

The gift of hospitality is a special ability God gives to certain members of the Body of Christ to provide food and lodging for those in need. A requirement for the use of this spiritual gift is that it is done without grudging. Grudging means resenting having to do it.

Hospitality is an evidence of unhypocritical love:

Let love be without dissimulation... given to hospitality... (Romans 12:9,13)

Hospitality is one of the qualifications of a bishop:

A bishop then must be...given to hospitality...(I Timothy 3:2)

For a bishop must be blameless...a lover of hospitality... (Titus 1:7-8)

FOR FURTHER STUDY:

Lydia is an example of one with the gift of hospitality: Acts 16:14-15

Gaius hosted Paul in Rome: Romans 16:23

There is an exciting possibility in showing hospitality. Discover what it is in Hebrews 13:1-2.

This happened to Abraham and Sarah: Genesis 18.

SELF-TEST

1. Write the Key Verse from memory.

____

____

2. List the nine serving gifts:

_______________ _______________

_______________ _______________

_______________ _______________

_______________ _______________

____

3. Why are these gifts called serving gifts?

____

____

4. What is the difference between the gifts of leadership and administration?

____

____

5. What is the difference between the gifts of helps and serving?

____

____

6. Read the list of serving gifts in list one. Read the definitions in list two. Write the number of the definition which describes the gift on the blank in front of it.

List One	**List Two**
_____Serving	1. Ability to evaluate people, doctrines, and situations as to whether they are of God.
_____Helps	2. Ability to motivate others to accomplish specific goals.
_____Leadership	3. Directs on behalf of others.
_____Administration	4. Special ability to believe.
_____Giving	5. Special ability to give.
_____Showing mercy	6. Assists others in their ministry.
_____Discerning of spirits	7. Special compassion.
_____Faith	8. Provides food and lodging.
_____Hospitality	9. Relieves others of responsibility to perform practical tasks.

7. Is this statement true or false: Only those with the gift of giving are required to give money to the work the Lord. The statement is:______________.

8. Define faith.

____

9. What is the difference between the gift of faith and the fruit of faith?

____

10. How can we increase our faith?

____

(Answers to tests are provided at the conclusion of the final chapter in this manual.)

FOR FURTHER STUDY

Suggestions for further study for each of the nine serving gifts were given as each gift was discussed. This was done to permit you to complete your study of each serving gift before going on to study the next one.

The Bible lists additional gifts which are given to believers which were not covered in this lesson. These gifts are not specifically called gifts of the Holy Spirit. For this reason they are not included in the study of spiritual gifts.

CELIBACY:

The gift of celibacy is the ability God gives to certain believers to remain single for the purpose of Christian service. In I Corinthians 7:7-8 the Apostle Paul refers to his gift of celibacy. Celibacy should not be required however (see I Timothy 4:1-5). It is a gift of God, not a requirement to be imposed by the church or a denomination. The church is edified by those who have the gift of celibacy (see I Corinthians 7:32-35).

INTERCESSION:

The gift of intercession is a special ability God gives to pray with great intensity for extended periods of time on a regular basis. To intercede means to plead on behalf of another. Intercessors pray for the needs of people, leaders, ministries, and nations.

Although intercession is not specifically identified as a spiritual gift, there is evidence that the Holy Spirit has provided for it to function as a gift (see Romans 8:26-27). Study the following passages to identify some of the purposes for intercessory prayer:

-James 5:14-16
-I Timothy 2:1-2
-Ephesians 6:19
-Numbers 14:17-19
-Acts 7:60

CRAFTSMANSHIP:

There is another gift which we will call "craftsmanship." It is the ability to craft things of beauty and/or function for the work of the Lord. Examples are seen in those given special skills by God to prepare items for the house of the Lord and garments for the priests (Exodus 28:3; Exodus 31:3-6).

CHAPTER NINE

SIGN GIFTS OF THE HOLY SPIRIT

OBJECTIVES:

Upon completion of this chapter you will be able to:

- Identify the four sign gifts of the Holy Spirit.
- Explain the purposes of miracles.
- Name five causes for physical illness.
- Distinguish between the gift of tongues and speaking in tongues as a physical sign of baptism in the Holy Spirit.
- Discuss Biblical guidelines governing use of the gift of tongues.

KEY VERSES:

> **How shall we escape, if we neglect so great salvation; which at the first began to be spoken by the Lord, and was confirmed unto us by them that heard Him;**
>
> **God also bearing them witness, both with signs and wonders, and with divers miracles, and gifts of the Holy Ghost, according to His own will? (Hebrews 2:3-4)**

INTRODUCTION

There are four gifts which we will call "sign gifts" because they are supernatural signs of God's power working through believers to confirm His Word:

> **And they went forth, and preached every where, the Lord working with them, and confirming the word with signs following. (Mark 16:20)**

The sign gifts minister to and through believers in healing, miracles, and special messages from God through tongues and interpretation. These supernatural gifts are also a "sign" to unbelievers that God exists.

The four sign gifts are:

-Miracles
-Healing
-Tongues
-Interpretation of tongues

MIRACLES

But the manifestation of the Spirit is given to every man to profit withal.

For to one is given by the Spirit...the working of miracles.
(I Corinthians 12:7-10)

Through a person with the gift of miracles God performs powerful acts which are beyond the possibility of occurring naturally. These supernatural acts are a sign that God's power is greater than that of Satan.

Miracles accomplish specific spiritual purposes. God uses miracles to confirm the Gospel message:

How shall we escape, if we neglect so great salvation; which at the first began to be spoken by the Lord, and was confirmed unto us by them that heard Him;

God also bearing them witness, both with signs and wonders, and with divers miracles and gifts of the Holy Ghost, according to His own will.
(Hebrews 2:3-4)

Miracles cause people to believe in Jesus and receive eternal life:

And many other signs truly did Jesus in the presence of His disciples, which are not written in this book:

But these are written that ye might believe that Jesus is the Christ, the Son of God; and that believing ye might have life through His name.
(John 20:30-31)

Miracles are also used by God to show approval of the person ministering. The ministry of Jesus was confirmed by miracles:

The same came to Jesus by night, and said unto him, Rabbi, we know that thou art a teacher come from God; for no man can do these miracles that thou doest, except God be with him. (John 3:2)

Ye men of Israel, hear these words; Jesus of Nazareth, a man approved of God among you by miracles and wonders and signs, which God did by Him in the midst of you, as ye yourselves also know. (Acts 2:22)

God confirmed the ministry of the apostles by miracles:

Truly the signs of an apostle were wrought among you in all patience, in signs, and wonders, and mighty deeds. (II Corinthians 12:12)

There are different types of miracles. Jesus demonstrated miraculous control over physical elements:

And He arose, and rebuked the wind, and said unto the sea, Peace, be still. And the wind ceased, and there was a great calm. (Mark 4:39)

Physical healing and the casting out of demons are miracles:

And God wrought special miracles by the hands of Paul:

So that from his body were brought unto the sick handkerchiefs or aprons and the diseases departed from them, and the evil spirits went out of them. (Acts 19:11-12)

The miracles by the hands of Paul were called "special miracles." The fact that they are called "special" to distinguish them from "ordinary" shows how common miracles were in the early church. The early church was birthed in a demonstration of great power. So common was the powerful manifestation of signs and wonders that this distinction was apparently necessary.

Signs and wonders do not necessarily mean a man or ministry is of God, however. Satan deceives through miracles:

For they are the spirits of devils, working miracles... (Revelation 16:14)

Even him, whose coming is after the working of Satan with all power and signs and lying wonders.

And with all deceivableness of unrighteousness in them that perish; because they received not the love of the truth, that they might be saved.

And for this cause God shall send them strong delusion that they should believe a lie:

That they all might be damned who believed not the truth, but had pleasure in unrighteousness. (II Thessalonians 2:9-12)

These verses indicate that people are deceived through miracles of Satan because they are not grounded in the truth of the Word of God.

FOR FURTHER STUDY:

1. Old Testament Miracles:

-Read the books of Exodus through Deuteronomy. See if you can identify the 26 miracles which occurred during the time of Moses.

-Read the books of I and II Kings. List the 21 miracles which occurred during the time of Elijah and Elisha.

2. New Testament Miracles:

-Study Matthew, Mark, Luke, and John. List the miracles performed by Jesus Christ.

-Study the book of Acts. List the miracles God performed through the apostles and others ministering in the early church.

-Read Acts 9:36-41. What miracle is recorded here? What are the results of this miracle (Acts 9:42)?

-According to Romans 15:18-19, what was evident in Paul's ministry which caused the Gentiles to become obedient to God?

-Read II Corinthians 12:12. With what other spiritual gift is the gift of miracles associated?

-What are two manifestations of miracles in Acts 19:11-12?

HEALING

But the manifestation of the Spirit is given to every man to profit withal.

For to one is given...the gifts of healing by the same Spirit. (I Corinthians 12:7-9)

A believer with the gifts of healing has the ability to let God's power flow through him to restore health apart from the use of natural methods. "Healing" means to make well.

This type of healing is called "divine healing" because it is done by the divine power of God rather than through natural means.

The healings recorded in the Bible were all immediate and complete recoveries of normal bodily functions. Physical healing is one of the spiritual signs that is to follow the ministry of all believers:

> **And these signs shall follow them that believe...they shall lay hands on the sick, and they shall recover... (Mark 16:17-18)**

The elders of the church are also used of God to bring physical healing:

> **Is any sick among you? Let him call for the elders of the church; and let them pray over him, anointing him with oil in the name of the Lord;**
>
> **And the prayer of faith shall save the sick, and the Lord shall raise him up; and if he have committed sins, they shall be forgiven him.**
> **(James 5:14-15)**

All believers can pray for the sick. Elders in the church can also pray for the sick. But a believer with a gift of healing is used specifically and consistently by God in this area of ministry.

The name of this gift is plural. It is the "gifts" of healing. This is because there are various healing gifts, different ways healing comes, and various methods of using the gift of healing. God uses some believers in the healing of specific illnesses. For example, the Bible records that Paul was used in special miracles of healing (Acts 19:11-12). Some believers may have a special anointing to pray for the blind or deaf. Others are used in a more general healing ministry to pray for all types of sickness.

In addition to curing physical affliction, healing can also include the casting out of unclean spirits [demons]:

> **There came also a multitude out of the cities round about unto Jerusalem, bringing sick folks, and them which were vexed with unclean spirits; and they were healed every one. (Acts 5:16)**

Faith in God is a key to receiving healing. Divine healing can come through the faith of the one ministering with this gift. Jesus raised a girl from the dead and healed her:

But when the people were put forth, He went in, and took her by the hand, and the maid arose. (Matthew 9:25)

Since the girl was dead, she could not have faith for healing. Healing came through the ministry and faith of Jesus.

Healing can also come because of the faith of the person who is sick:

But Jesus turned Him about and when He saw her, He said, Daughter, be of good comfort; thy faith hath made thee whole. And the woman was made whole from that hour. (Matthew 9:22)

Healing also comes through the combined faith of the one who is sick and the one who is ministering:

And when He was come into the house, the blind men came to Him: and Jesus saith unto them, Believe ye that I am able to do this? They said unto Him Yea, Lord.

Then touched He their eyes, saying, According to your faith be it unto you. (Matthew 9:28-29)

Jesus had the ability to perform this healing. He knew He was able to heal. This was combined with the faith of the blind men to bring healing.

The plural "gifts" of healing is also used because healing comes through various Biblical methods. For example, healing can come through the spoken word:

The centurion answered and said, Lord, I am not worthy that thou shouldest come under my roof: but speak the word only, and my servant shall be healed. (Matthew 8:8)

He sent His word, and healed them... (Psalms 107:20)

Healing comes by the laying on of hands:

Now when the sun was setting, all they that had any sick with divers diseases brought them unto Him; and He laid His hands on every one of them, and healed them. (Luke 4:40)

...they shall lay hands on the sick, and they shall recover... (Mark 16:18)

And God wrought special miracles by the hands of Paul. (Acts 19:11)

Healing comes through the anointing of oil in the name of the Lord:

Is any sick among you? let him call for the elders of the church; and let them pray over him, anointing him with oil in the name of the Lord;

And the prayer of faith shall save the sick, and the Lord shall raise him up; and if he have committed sins, they shall be forgiven him. (James 5:14-15)

Healing has even come through the shadow of one with this gift:

Insomuch that they brought forth the sick into the streets, and laid them on beds and couches, that at the least the shadow of Peter passing by might overshadow some of them.

There came also a multitude out of the cities round about unto Jerusalem, bringing sick folks, and them which were vexed with unclean spirits; and they were healed every one. (Acts 5:15-16)

We can have divine healing because Jesus suffered and took upon Himself our infirmities:

But He was wounded for our transgressions, He was bruised for our iniquities; the chastisement of our peace was upon Him; and with His stripes we are healed. (Isaiah 53:5)

Jesus suffered at Calvary not only to free us from sin, but also to free us from sickness. He was beaten and received stripes on His back for the healing of sickness. He suffered so we can be healed as well as saved.

When ministering with the gifts of healing it is important to understand that everyone to whom we minister may not be healed. Paul spoke of fellow workers who were sick and apparently had not received healing through his ministry:

...Trophimus have I left at Miletum sick. (II Timothy 4:20)

Paul had the gifts of healing and special miracles, yet for some reason Trophimus was not healed through his ministry. Paul wrote to Timothy regarding a chronic illness:

Drink no longer water, but use a little wine for thy stomach's sake and thine often infirmities. (I Timothy 5:23)

Paul did not stop using his gift of healing just because everyone to whom he ministered did not get healed. This would be like an evangelist ceasing to minister because everyone to whom he preached did not respond to the Gospel. Everyone Paul preached to did not respond positively to the Gospel message. Everyone he prayed for was not healed. But he kept on doing what God had called him to do. He preached the Gospel and prayed for the sick and left the results in the hands of God.

There are reasons why healing does not come to everyone for whom we pray. These are discussed in the Harvestime International Institute course entitled *"Leaven-Like Evangelism,"* which deals with healing in detail and its purpose in extending the Gospel.

FOR FURTHER STUDY:

-For a detailed study of healing, obtain the Harvestime International Institute course entitled *"Battle For The Body."*

-Read Matthew, Mark, Luke, and John to study the healing ministry of Jesus. Make a list of all the healings He performed. By each healing, record the different methods used.

-Read the book of Acts to study the gifts of healing in action in the early church. Note the types of sickness healed and the methods used.

Observe in the book of Acts the different people God used in the gifts of healing:

-Acts 3:1-11:	Peter and John [apostles]
-Acts 5:15; 9:32-34:	Peter [apostle]
-Acts 8:5-7:	Philip [evangelist and deacon]
-Acts 9:17-18:	Ananias [unknown believer]
-Acts 14:8-10; 28:7-9:	Paul [apostle]

-Study the following verses. Make a list of some of the reasons God performs healings: John 9:1-3; Acts 3:1-10; 4:4; Philippians 2:25-27

TONGUES

But the manifestation of the Spirit is given to every man to profit withal.

**For to one is given by the Spirit...divers kinds of tongues...
(I Corinthians 12:7-10)**

The gift of tongues is the ability to receive and communicate a message of God to His people through a language never learned. "Tongues" means languages. The reason we have called this a "sign" gift rather than a "speaking" gift is that the Bible indicates clearly that this gift is given for a sign.

When one speaks in tongues it can be in a language known and recognized by the listeners:

Now when this was noised abroad, the multitude came together, and were confounded, because that every man heard them speak in his own language...

And they were all amazed and marvelled, saying one to another, Behold are not all these which speak Galilaeans?

And how hear we every man in our own tongue, wherein we were born. (Acts 2:6-8)

It can also be in a language not known to man. This is called speaking in unknown tongues:

For he that speaketh in an unknown tongue speaketh not unto men, but unto God; for no man understandeth him; howbeit in the Spirit he speaketh mysteries. (I Corinthians 14:2)

As you previously learned, speaking in tongues is the physical sign of having been baptized in the Holy Spirit. But this experience of speaking in tongues is different from the gift of tongues. The gift of tongues is the special ability to deliver messages from God to the church in a language not known by the speaker.

The purposes of speaking in tongues, both as a sign of baptism in the Holy Spirit and the gift of tongues are for:

Prayer to God: I Corinthians 14:2

Self edification: I Corinthians 14:4. Edification is not exalting self, but means encouragement, improvement, and development. Isaiah 28:11-12 also calls it spiritual refreshing.

Intercession: The Holy Spirit speaks through the believer in an unknown tongue to intercede in prayer. The word "intercede" means to pray on behalf of another. The Holy Spirit knows just how and for what to pray. I Corinthians 14:14. See also Romans 8:26,27

Praise: Acts 10:46; I Corinthians 14:15

Fulfillment of prophecy: I Corinthians 14:21; Isaiah 28:11-12

The gift of tongues has two additional purposes. When a person with the gift of tongues gives a message to the church assembly and this message is interpreted it is for...

Edification of the church: I Corinthians 14:12-13

A sign to unbelievers: I Corinthians 14:22. This is why the gift of tongues and the interpretation which should accompany use of this gift are called "sign gifts."

There are specific guidelines given for using the gift of tongues in the church:

1. Not everyone is to speak at one time: I Corinthians 12:30

2. To edify the church, the gift of tongues must be accompanied by interpretation so the listeners will understand what is said: I Corinthians 14:1-5

3. Because of this, a believer with the gift of tongues should keep quiet if there is no interpreter: I Corinthians 14:28

4. He should also pray for the gift of interpretation himself: I Corinthians 12:13

5. In the church it is more important to speak in language understood than tongues if no interpreter is present: I Corinthians 14:18-19

6. Only one person should interpret at a time: I Corinthians 14:27

7. A person with the gift of tongues can control it: I Corinthians 14:32-33

8. Speaking in tongues is not to be forbidden: I Corinthians 14:39-40

9. The most important thing is order in the church services. There should be no confusion caused by this or any other gift: I Corinthians 14:40

FOR FURTHER STUDY:

-Study I Corinthians 12-14. These chapters discuss the use of spiritual gifts with emphasis on the gifts of tongues and interpretation in chapter 14.

-Read I Corinthians 14:5. With what gift is tongues, when interpreted, compared?

-What are the purposes of this gift? See I Corinthians 14:4,5,22.

-What guidelines are placed on the use of this gift in the assembled church? See I Corinthians 14:26-28.

-The gift of tongues is a sign to unbelievers. For each passage listed discover who the unbelievers were and where they were from:

	Who	**Where From**
Acts 2:2-13	_______________	_____________________
Acts 10:24-28	_______________	_____________________
Acts 19:1-7	_______________	_____________________

INTERPRETATION OF TONGUES

> **But the manifestation of the Spirit is given to every man to profit withal.**
>
> **For to one is given by the Spirit the...interpretation of tongues. (I Corinthians 12:7-10)**

The gift of interpretation is a special ability to make known in a language understood the message of one who speaks in tongues. The interpretation of a message in tongues is given by the Holy Spirit to one with this spiritual gift. It is not interpreted by knowing the language in which the message was given. It is given by revelation from the Holy Spirit. Interpretation is a summary of the message, not a word by word translation. Because of this, interpretation may vary from the message in tongues in length or structure.

The purpose of this gift is to provide interpretation of the message given by one with the gift of tongues:

> **If any man speak in an unknown tongue, let it be by two, or at the most by three, and that by course; and let one interpret. (I Corinthians 14:27)**

The gift of interpretation is to accompany use of the gift of tongues. It is only when a message in tongues is interpreted that the church is blessed by it:

> **I would that ye all spake with tongues, but rather that ye prophesied; for greater is he that prophesieth than he that speaketh with tongues, except he interpret that the church may receive edifying. (I Corinthians 14:5)**

A person with the gift of tongues is to keep silent in the church if there is no one present with the gift of interpretation:

> **But if there be no interpreter, let him keep silence in the church; and let him speak to himself, and to God. (I Corinthians 14:28)**

A person with the gift of tongues should pray for the gift of interpretation:

Wherefore let him that speaketh in an unknown tongue pray that he may interpret. (I Corinthians 14:13)

FOR FURTHER STUDY:

-Study I Corinthians 14 for further guidelines on using the gift of interpretation of tongues.
-What should be the results when tongues are interpreted? See I Corinthians 14:5
-What is to happen if no interpreter is present? See I Corinthians 14:28.
-Who interprets the tongues? See I Corinthians 14:13 and 27.
-On what occasions does the gift of tongues not require interpretation? See Acts 2:4-8; 10:44-48;19:6.

THE PATTERN OF EFFECTIVE MINISTRY

This chapter concludes the study of the various spiritual gifts. The divisions made for purposes of study were:

-Special gifts	-Speaking gifts
-Serving gifts	-Sign gifts

The following chart shows how each of these divisions fit together in the church to form a pattern of effective ministry:

SPECIAL GIFTS

Apostles
Prophets ⇒ TO EQUIP GOD'S PEOPLE
Evangelists

Pastors
Teachers

SPEAKING GIFTS

TO EXPLAIN GOD'S TRUTHS ⇒

Prophecy
Teaching
Exhortation
Word of Wisdom
Word of Knowledge

SERVING GIFTS

Serving
Helps
Leadership
Administration
Giving ⇒ TO ENABLE GOD'S WORK
Showing Mercy
Discerning of Spirits
Faith
Hospitality

SIGN GIFTS

TO ESTABLISH GOD'S AUTHORITY ⇒

Tongues
Interpretation
Miracles
Healings

SELF-TEST

1. Write the Key Verses from memory.

____

____

2. What are the four sign gifts?

____

____

____

____

3. According to John 20:30-31, what are two purposes of the gift of miracles?

____

____

4. Look at the sign gift in list one. Read the definitions in list two. Write the number of the definition that describes the gift in the blank provided.

List One	**List Two**
_____Healing	1. Powerful acts beyond the possibility of occurring naturally.
_____Tongues	2. God's power restoring health apart from the use of natural methods.
_____Interpretation	3. Speaking in a language not known by the speaker.
_____Miracles	4. Making known in a language understood the message of one who speaks in tongues.

5. Read the statements below. If the statement is TRUE, write a T on the blank in front of it. If the statement is FALSE, write an F on the blank in front of it.

a.______Speaking in tongues upon baptism in the Holy Spirit is the same thing as the gift of tongues.

b.______A person with the gift of tongues should keep quiet in the church if there is no interpreter present.

c.______A person with the gift of tongues should not interpret his own message.

d.______A person with the gift of tongues can not really control this gift.

e.______It is more important to speak in a language understood by listeners in the church than to speak with the gift of tongues with no interpretation.

f.______Several people can interpret the same message at the same time.

g.______If a person has the gifts of healing, everyone to whom he ministers will be healed.

h.______Only a person with the gifts of healing should pray for the sick.

((Answers to tests are provided at the conclusion of the final chapter in this manual.)

FOR FURTHER STUDY

Suggestions for further study for each of the four sign gifts were given as each gift was discussed. This was done to permit you to complete your study of each sign gift before going on to the next one. A final suggestion is that you learn how all the gifts of the Holy Spirit were evident in the ministry of Jesus Christ. The following outline will assist you in this as it lists references confirming spiritual gifts evident in His ministry.

After you conclude this study read the books of Matthew, Mark, Luke, and John. Expand this outline by listing other references which confirm the operation of the gifts in the ministry of Jesus Christ.

GIFTS OF THE HOLY SPIRIT IN THE LIFE OF JESUS

-Miracles:	Acts 2:22
-Healing:	Acts 10:38
-Word Of Wisdom:	I Corinthians 1:24,30
-Word Of Knowledge:	John 1:45-50; 4:18; 11:14
-Discerning of Spirits:	John 1:45-50 6:61
-Prophecy/Prophet:	Matthew 24
-Teaching/Teacher:	Matthew 4:23; 9:35; 26:55; Mark 6:6; 14:49; Luke 5:17; 13:10,22; 21:37
-Exhortation:	Luke 3:18
-Mercy [compassion]:	Matthew 20:30-34
-Apostle:	Hebrews 3:1
-Evangelist:	John 10:16
-Pastor:	John 10:11
-Leadership:	John 13:15-16; Mark 10:42-45
-Administration:	Luke 10:1-17
-Faith:	Luke 8:49-56
-Giving:	John 10:11
-Helps:	John 17:6-10
-Serving:	John 13:4-16; Mark 10:42-45
-Hospitality:	John 21:9-13 [Had no home yet had hospitality].

-Tongues and Interpretation: These were the only two spiritual gifts not evident in the life of Jesus. These were not necessary because He was the Word of God Himself. There was no need for the gifts of tongues and interpretation to bring a message from God through Him to man.

CHAPTER TEN

DISCOVERING YOUR SPIRITUAL GIFT

OBJECTIVES:

Upon completion of this chapter you will be able to:

- Explain why it is important for a believer to discover his spiritual gift.
- Explain how a believer can discover his spiritual gift.
- Discover your own spiritual gift.

KEY VERSE:

> **Wherefore I put thee in remembrance that thou stir up the gift of God, which is in thee by the putting on of my hands. (II Timothy 1:6)**

INTRODUCTION

In previous chapters you learned that each believer has at least one spiritual gift. This chapter explains how to discover and begin to use your spiritual gift.

THE IMPORTANCE OF DISCOVERY

It is important to discover your spiritual gift in order to:

ACCOMPLISH SPIRITUAL PURPOSES AND OBJECTIVES:

You will recall the purposes and objectives of gifts of the Holy Spirit given in Ephesians 4:12-15:

Purposes:

-Perfect the saints.
-Promote the work of the ministry.
-Edify Christ and the church.

Objectives:

-We will become united in the faith.
-We will develop our knowledge of Christ.
-We will develop in perfection, with Christ as our model.
-We will become stable, not deceived by false doctrines.
-We will mature spiritually in Christ.

If these purposes and objectives are to be accomplished in the church then it is necessary that each believer discover and use his spiritual gift.

CONDUCT SPIRITUAL WARFARE:

The gifts of the Holy Spirit are also given to the church as weapons of spiritual warfare to fight the spiritual forces of Satan:

> **For we wrestle not against flesh and blood, but against principalities, against powers, against the rulers of the darkness of this world, against spiritual wickedness in high places. (Ephesians 6:12)**

It is important to discover and use your spiritual gift in order to effectively fight your spiritual enemy, Satan.

AVOID ABUSES:

In previous chapters you learned there are three ways spiritual gifts can be abused:

1. Not using those gifts given to you.
2. Attempting to use gifts not given to you.
3. Not using the gifts properly.

It is important to discover your spiritual gift in order to avoid these abuses.

AVOID FRUSTRATION:

Many new believers often plunge into ministry without knowing their spiritual gifts, experiencing frustration and defeat as they try to work for the Lord. You, too, will be frustrated if you do not discover your own spiritual gift. You will be ineffective if you try to serve in positions for which God has not given you a gift to minister.

You may be busy in ministry, but you will not be accomplishing anything for the Kingdom of God. For example, one person tried to imitate the gift of a great evangelist named Billy Graham. He preached just like Rev. Graham but no one responded to his messages. He was very frustrated in the ministry until he discovered that his spiritual gift was not the gift of evangelism. His gift was teaching. When he began to use his own gift of teaching he saw great results in his ministry.

Discovering your spiritual gift will not only keep you from being frustrated with yourself, it will also keep you from being frustrated with other Christians. For example, you will understand if your pastor is a good teacher but a poor administrator. You will recognize that he has the gift of teaching but does not have the gift of administration. Instead of criticism, he needs the help of someone who does have this gift in order for the church to operate more efficiently.

ASSUME YOUR RESPONSIBILITY:

It is important to discover your spiritual gift because you have a responsibility to "stir up" and use it. The Apostle Paul wrote Timothy:

> **Neglect not the gift that is in thee...(I Timothy 4:14)**
>
> **Wherefore I put thee in remembrance that thou stir up the gift of God, which is in thee by the putting on of my hands. (II Timothy 1:6)**

You must discover your spiritual gift in order to fulfill your responsibility to develop it. You must know your gift in order to set priorities which permit you to use it productively.

DISCOVERING YOUR SPIRITUAL GIFT

The following guidelines will help you discover your spiritual gift or gifts:

STEP ONE - Be Born Again:

You must be born again. Spiritual gifts come through the new birth just as natural talents come through natural physical birth. If you are never born in the natural world you will not have natural talents. If you are not born again in the spiritual world you cannot be given spiritual gifts:

> **Repent, and be baptized every one of you in the name of Jesus Christ for the remission of sins, and ye shall receive the gift of the Holy Ghost. (Acts 2:38)**

STEP TWO - Receive The Baptism Of The Holy Spirit:

Guidelines for how to receive the baptism of the Holy Spirit were given in Chapter Four of this manual.

STEP THREE - Know The Spiritual Gifts:

If you do not know what spiritual gifts exist, you will not be able to recognize the one(s) God has given you. The lessons you studied in this course have equipped you to identify the various gifts available to believers.

STEP FOUR - Observe Models Of The Gifts:

As you are considering what gifts you might have, it is helpful to observe mature models of the various gifts. A "mature model" of a spiritual gift is a believer who has been effectively using a gift for an extended period of time.

For example, talk with someone who has the gift of teaching. Question them as to how they knew they had the gift, how they began to use it, and ways they are continuing to develop their gift. Do the same for the other gifts. Learning how others discovered their gifts and observing mature models of the gifts in action will help you identify your own gift.

STEP FIVE - Seek A Spiritual Gift:

Desire a gift and fast and pray for it. The Bible tells us to seek spiritual gifts:

> **But covet [desire, seek] earnestly the best gifts... (I Corinthians 12:31)**

We each have at least one gift, but this verse implies we can also seek a gift which we do not now possess.

STEP SIX - Laying On Of Hands:

Have your spiritual leader lay hands on you and pray for God to reveal your spiritual gift:

> **Neglect not the gift that is in thee, which was given thee by prophecy, with the laying on of the hands of the presbytery. (I Timothy 4:14)**

Note: As a result of Steps One through Six God may reveal your spiritual gift. If this does not happen, proceed with the following steps.

STEP SEVEN - Analyze Your Spiritual Interests:

The areas in which you find great joy in serving God are often those for which He has gifted you. Just as a gift you receive in the natural world brings joy, so do spiritual gifts. You must have a "passion" or "burden" [great interest or desire] for a certain ministry in order to serve God effectively.

For example, a person with the gift of administration can use it to organize and direct anything. He could administer a church, a Christian school, a drug rehabilitation center, etc. But he must have a burden or passion for the ministry where he uses his gift. If he has no interest in a Christian school, he will not last long even though he has the gift of administration.

Answer the following questions to help determine your spiritual interest or burden:

1. What kind or group of people do you feel most attracted to?

____

(If you are called to a particular group of people, your spiritual gift will relate to their need. For example, if you feel a call to children and want to see them learn about God, you may have the gift of teaching).

2. What areas of need cause a strong emotional stirring in you?

____

(When God calls you to meet a specific need, you will often feel a strong emotional stirring within).

3. If you could not fail, what would you desire to do for the Lord?

____

(God honors personal desires).

4. Complete this sentence: "I have a growing restless conviction from within that I should get involved in..."

____

(Such convictions are often God speaking to your spirit about an area in which He wants you to serve).

5. I am certain God has definitely called me to a specific area of ministry. It is...

____

(If you know the specific area of ministry to which God has called you, it will be easy to determine your spiritual gift. God always provides the necessary gifts to enable you to fulfill the call. The "For Further Study" section of this lesson will assist you in recognizing your spiritual calling).

6. What gifts bring you the most joy in thinking about them or using them? (For example, do you enjoy teaching? Do you enjoy being hospitable and having people into your home? Are you often moved to give large sums of money to God's work?)

____

STEP EIGHT - Analysis By A Christian Leader:

Have a Christian leader analyze your spiritual abilities. Ask the following questions and record the answers:

1. In what areas of Christian service have you observed me to be effective?

____

2. Based upon this observation of my effectiveness, what spiritual gifts do you believe I might have?

____

STEP NINE - Analyze Your Past Christian Service:

Analyze your past ministry. Answer these questions:

1. In what areas of Christian service have you ministered in the past?

____

2. In which of these were you effective?

____

3. In which of these did you experience great joy in serving?

____

4. In which of these did your spiritual leader and/or others note your effectiveness?

____

STEP TEN - Complete The Spiritual Gift Questionnaires:

The final part of this lesson contains two spiritual gift questionnaires. Your answers to these questions will help you identify spiritual gifts which you may have.

STEP ELEVEN - Identify Gifts You Think You Might Have:

Identify the gifts you think you might have based on:

1. The knowledge of gifts you have obtained through study.
2. What God has revealed to you through prayer.
3. hat you have analyzed in yourself.
4. What a key Christian leader has observed in your life.
5. Analysis of your effectiveness in areas of ministry in which you have previously served.
6. Completion of the Spiritual Gifts Questionnaires.

A list of the gifts is provided in "Step Thirteen" which follows. Put an x by the gift(s) you believe you might have.

STEP TWELVE - Identify Spiritual Needs:

Analyze the spiritual needs of your neighborhood, community, and church. Review this list of needs:

Visitation: Sick, newcomers to church, members of church, hospital, widows, prisons, bereaved, home for aged.

Evangelism: House-to-house, evangelistic services, crusades, open air services.

Follow Up Ministry: To new converts.

Counseling: General counseling or to specific groups; telephone counseling.

Office/administrative Support: Typing, drawing [art], filing, assembling, reproducing materials, mailings, telephones, records.

Hospitality: Cooking meals and lodging for those in need or for visiting ministers, evangelists, Christians.

Ministry To Poor: Providing food, clothing, shelter.

Maintenance Of Church Buildings: Landscaping, painting, carpentry, electrical, plumbing, cleaning.

Music: Choir, instruments, song leader, special music groups, soloist, writing music.

Religious Dramatic Productions. Writing or producing Christian dramas.

Financial: Fund raising, accounting, financial planning for ministries.

Writing: Christian books, newsletters, tracts, news and magazine articles, poetry.

Multi-media: Audio and video tapes, radio, television, satellite.

Ministry To Special Groups: Deaf, blind, mentally ill, narcotic addicts, alcoholics, migrant workers, gangs, unwed mothers, homosexuals, Jews, minority groups, women, men, families, married couples, abused children, runaways, school dropouts, illiterate, prisoners, military, children, youth, aged.

Church Offices: Elder, deacon/deaconness, Sunday school teacher, usher, committees such as building, finance, etc.

Translation: Bible and Christian literature.

Christian Education: Sunday school, vacation Bible school, Christian preschool, elementary, high school, college; training for laymen using Harvestime International Institute courses, home Bible studies.

Missionary/Church Planting: To unreached peoples in your region/nation.

Literature: Christian library, bookstore, Bible and Christian literature distribution.

Camps And Retreats.

Now, answer these questions:

1. What needs are not being met in your neighborhood?

____

2. What needs are not being met in your community?

____

3. What needs are not being met in your church?

____

STEP THIRTEEN - Fill A Spiritual Need:

The analysis you have completed will be of no benefit unless you apply it to your life and ministry. To "apply" something means to use it effectively, to actually do something with it.

Compare the list of spiritual needs you made in "Step Twelve" to the list of gifts you believe God has given you. Identify a spiritual need that corresponds with the gift you believe you have, then make a commitment to fill this need. For example, if there is a need for teachers in your church and you believe you have the gift of teaching, volunteer to meet this need. Use the form provided on the following page:

Matching Spiritual Gifts With Needs

I believe I have the spiritual gift(s) marked below:	Needs This Gift Can Meet In My Neighborhood	Community	Church
___Apostle			
___Prophet			
___Evangelist			
___Pastor			
___Teacher			
___Prophecy			
___Teaching			
___Exhortation			
___Word of Wisdom			
___Word of Knowledge			
___Serving			

I believe I have the spiritual gift(s) marked below	Needs This Gift Can Meet In My Neighborhood	Community	Church
___Helps			
___Leadership			
___Administration			
___Giving			
___Showing Mercy			
___Discerning of Spirits			

___Faith ____
___Hospitality ____
___Tongues ____
___Interpretation ____
___Miracles ____
___Healings ____

STEP FOURTEEN - Evaluate Your Ministry:

After serving awhile in this area with your gift, evaluate your ministry. You have discovered and are showing proper stewardship of your spiritual gift...

-When you are fruitful in the area in which you are serving. This means you will see positive results of your ministry.

-When you are fulfilled...you are enjoying your ministry. If you are frustrated, you may not be serving in an area for which you are gifted.

-When the feedback [comments you receive from your spiritual leaders] indicate you are effective in the position in which you are serving.

If the ministry you are filling does not fit your spiritual capabilities and you are ineffective, review your list of possible gifts and ask God to show you another area in which to minister.

Do not be discouraged...Remember the man who thought he was an evangelist but later discovered he was a teacher! It is just as important to know what gifts you do not have as to discover the gift you do have. This prevents you from wasting your life in ministry where you will not be effective. By combining prayer and these practical steps you will soon discover that special place of ministry God has for you. As you begin to serve, you will quickly discover your giftedness.

SELF-TEST

1. Write the Key Verse from memory.

____

____

____

2. List five reasons why it is important to discover your spiritual gift.

____

____

____

____

____

3. List fourteen steps that will help you discover your spiritual gift.

____________________	____________________
____________________	____________________
____________________	____________________
____________________	____________________
____________________	____________________
____________________	____________________
____________________	____________________

(Answers to tests are provided at the conclusion of the final chapter in this manual.)

FOR FURTHER STUDY

1. God always provides the gifts necessary to enable you to fulfill your spiritual calling. How can you know if you are called? Study the following pattern demonstrated in the call of Moses:

God Provides The Direction:

Read Exodus 3:1-4. The first principle of recognizing a call from God is to understand that God takes the initiative. He has the responsibility to communicate to you what He wants you to do.

You do not have to run around in frustration trying to find out what God wants you to do. You do not have to take an opinion poll among your friends to see what they think you should do. It is God's responsibility to clearly communicate His call to you. Your responsibility is to fulfill that call once it has been given. A true call from God is not something you decide to do on your own or that others think you should do.

You Will Have A Burden:

For years, Moses had a deep burden in his heart for his people, Israel. He felt so strongly about this that he had even murdered an Egyptian and that is why he was in the wilderness (Exodus 2:11-15). When you are called by God to a specific ministry, you will feel a deep burden, interest, concern, and compassion in that area.

You Will Receive A God-Given Plan:

Burden, interest, concern, and compassion alone are not enough to fulfill the call of God. In addition to providing direction and burden, God will communicate a plan to enable you to fulfill your calling.

Here is where many people fail. They receive a call and a burden from God, but they rush off to try to fulfill this call without waiting for God to communicate His plan.

God gave Moses a plan. He and Aaron were to appear before Pharaoh and gain the release of the Israelites. They were then to lead them through the wilderness to the land which God had promised them. When God gives you a call and a burden, wait until you receive His plan for fulfilling your ministry.

You Will Have A Sense Of Inadequacy:

In Exodus 3:8, you can readily see the inadequacy Moses felt. He said "Who am I, that I should go unto Pharaoh, and that I should bring forth the children of Israel out of Egypt?"

When you receive a true call from God, you will always feel inadequate. (If you feel self-sufficient for a task...be careful. It most likely is not a true call from God!) When God calls you, you will sense weakness, inadequacy, and need. You will not feel qualified to do what He has called you to do, and you will be overwhelmed by the challenge.

You are in good company! Great men and women of God throughout the centuries have felt the same way. But those who fulfilled their calling despite their inadequacies believed God was adequate. God answered Moses in Exodus 3:12, saying ."..certainly I will be with thee." God is not looking for those who feel self-sufficient. It is not who you are that is important, but who God is!

2. Study the lives of other Bible personalities and you will discover this same pattern in their call from God. For examples, read about the call of Gideon in Judges 6 and the call of Jeremiah in Jeremiah l.

3. The following checklist will assist you in completing the practical steps for discovering your spiritual gift which were given in this chapter:

Step One: _____I have been born again.

Step Two: _____I have received the baptism of the Holy Spirit.

Step Three: _____I can identify the various spiritual gifts.

Step Four: _____I have observed mature models of the gifts.

Step Five: _____I have sought a spiritual gift by fasting and prayer.

Step Six: _____I have had my spiritual leaders lay hands on me and ask God to reveal my gift(s).

Step Seven: _____I have analyzed my spiritual interests.

Step Eight: _____I have been analyzed by my spiritual leader.

Step Nine: _____I have analyzed my past Christian service.

Step Ten: _____I have completed the spiritual gift questionnaires.

Step Eleven: _____I have identified the spiritual gifts I believe I might have.

Step Twelve: _____I have identified spiritual needs in my home, community, and church.

Step Thirteen: _____I have matched my gift to a need and begun to fill it.

Step Fourteen: _____I have evaluated my ministry in this area and found it to be effective.

SPIRITUAL GIFT QUESTIONNAIRES

There are two different questionnaires. One is for the Special Gifts of apostle, prophet, evangelist, pastor, and teacher. The other is for the remaining Spiritual Gifts. You complete each questionnaire in the same way by marking either a YES or NO answer to each question.

Here Is An Example:

YES NO

(x) ( ) 1. Do you believe that God is calling you to a place of leadership?

SPECIAL GIFTS

SPECIAL GIFTS QUESTIONNAIRE:

This particular test on "Special Gifts" (apostle, prophet, evangelist, pastor, and teacher) is designed to help you to evaluate whether your desires and patterns of life are manifesting the qualifications and characteristics of these gifted people. While this test may be helpful, it cannot be considered conclusive. You must carefully evaluate the inward call of God, the continual and effective use of the gift, and the confirmation of that gift by other members of the body of Christ.

YES	NO		
( )	( )	1.	Do you believe God is calling you to a place of leadership?
( )	( )	2.	Have you ever desired to be a missionary?
( )	( )	3.	Do you believe God has given you the ability to be a public speaker?
( )	( )	4.	Do you have a great desire to witness to un believers?
( )	( )	5.	Do you enjoy spending time in Bible study?
( )	( )	6.	Have you had a continual desire to be in the full-time ministry of the Word of God?
( )	( )	7.	Do you enjoy moving from place to place frequently?
( )	( )	8.	Do you feel capable of speaking in front of large audiences?
( )	( )	9.	Do you enjoy sharing the Gospel with unbelievers more than teaching and training Christians?
( )	( )	10.	Would you rather work in a local church than move to another place with new opportunities?
( )	( )	11.	Do you believe your marriage and family background would be an example for others to follow?
( )	( )	12.	Do you feel gifted in terms of developing leaders for the church?
( )	( )	13.	When you see conditions and situations that are not right, do you desire to be involved in correcting them?
( )	( )	14.	Is witnessing to unbelievers easy for you?
( )	( )	15.	Do you enjoy relationships with people with whom you are not well acquainted?
( )	( )	16.	Would other people who know you well describe you as a patient and kind person?
( )	( )	17.	Have you ever started a ministry for the Lord and watched it grow to the point that others were trained to do what you were doing?
( )	( )	18.	Do you frequently sense a spirit of boldness in wanting to speak God's Word to people and situations where it is needed?
( )	( )	19.	Do you witness more out of a desire than out of responsibility and duty?

YES	NO		
( )	( )	20.	Do you like working with people, dealing with their personal problems, burdens, and questions, more than letting others take this responsibility?
( )	( )	21.	Would you describe yourself as a well-disciplined person?
( )	( )	22.	Would you find it easy to go and live in another country or culture?
( )	( )	23.	Have other believers commented that when you speak God's Word to people they feel convicted?
( )	( )	24.	Has anyone ever shared with you that you seem to be gifted in evangelism?
( )	( )	25.	Would you enjoy having a regular teaching ministry that would involve believers at all levels of maturity?
( )	( )	26.	Would you describe yourself as a person of hospitality, who enjoys having people in your home?
( )	( )	27.	Do you find it relatively easy to endure hardship in the midst of difficult and changing circumstances?
( )	( )	28.	Do you find yourself being aggressive in sharing God's Word with people in need rather than waiting to be asked?
( )	( )	29.	Do you find a greater interest and concern in reaching the unsaved for Christ than in teaching and training believers?
( )	( )	30.	Do you feel a burden to train believers in how to use their spiritual gifts and minister effectively for the Lord?
( )	( )	31.	Are you a person who is able to live with financial pressure and limited income without emotional stress and a desire to make more money?
( )	( )	32.	Are you presently free from family and financial responsibilities that might keep you from moving to another country or culture?
( )	( )	33.	Are you more inclined toward public speaking than private conversation?
( )	( )	34.	Do you find yourself actively seeking opportunities to witness for Christ?
( )	( )	35.	Are you comfortable spending long hours in research and study of the Bible?
( )	( )	36.	Have you been a Christian for more than three years?
( )	( )	37.	Do you believe you are capable of winning people to Christ and training them to become pastors?
( )	( )	38.	Have you had experience in preaching God's Word to groups who were gathered together to hear you speak?
( )	( )	39.	Do you begin each day with an anticipation and desire to share the Gospel with an unbeliever?

YES NO

( ) ( ) 40. Has anyone ever told you that you would make a good pastor or teacher?

( ) ( ) 41. Have you had the responsibility of managing a family or a business that other people would say has been successful?

( ) ( ) 42. Do you find it easy to meet strangers and get acquainted with them quickly?

( ) ( ) 43. Do you frequently become concerned about moral issues in various situations, desiring to speak out against that which is wrong?

( ) ( ) 44. Do you have frequent conversations with unbelievers about the Person and work of Jesus Christ?

( ) ( ) 45. Do you believe God has given you the ability to work with people and their problems in a positive and loving manner?

( ) ( ) 46. Are you convinced that other believers would say you are a gifted leader for the church?

( ) ( ) 47. Is it easy for you to turn over responsibilities to others who demonstrate
leadership abilities?

( ) ( ) 48. Would others describe you as an effective public speaker?

( ) ( ) 49. Would you say that you have such a burden for unbelievers to be saved that it often controls what you do and say?

( ) ( ) 50. Would you enjoy having the responsibility of caring for all the spiritual needs of a group of people?

SPECIAL GIFTS SCORING SHEET:

When you have finished the questionnaire, complete the next page. For each question which you marked YES on the questionnaire, make a mark in the box by that question number. DO NOT MAKE ANY MARKS FOR NO ANSWERS. Make a mark for only those questions which you answered with a YES answer.

Here Is An Example: This person marked YES to questions 1, 6, and 13, so he marks the boxes by these numbers on the answer sheet:

GENERAL QUALIFICATIONS (Applies to all four gifted persons)	PROPHET (Preacher)
(x) #1	( ) #3
(x) #6	( ) #8
( ) #11	(x) #13

He answered questions 11, 3, and 8 with NO, so he does <u>not</u> make any marks by these numbers on the answer sheet. Now, record your own scores:

GENERAL QUALIFICATIONS
(Applies to all four
gifted persons)

( ) #1
( ) #6
( ) #11
( ) #16
( ) #21
( ) #26
( ) #31
( ) #36
( ) #41
( ) #46

PROPHET
(Preacher)

( ) #3
( ) #8
( ) #13
( ) #18
( ) #23
( ) #28
( ) #33
( ) #38
( ) #43
( ) #48

APOSTLE
(Missionary)

( ) #2
( ) #7
( ) #12
( ) #17
( ) #22
( ) #27
( ) #32
( ) #37
( ) #42
( ) #47

EVANGELIST

( ) #4
( ) #9
( ) #14
( ) #19
( ) #24
( ) #29
( ) #34
( ) #39
( ) #44
( ) #49

PASTOR TEACHER

( ) #5
( ) #10
( ) #15
( ) #20
( ) #25
( ) #30
( ) #35
( ) #40
( ) #45
( ) #50

SPECIAL GIFTS PROFILE:

Using the scoring sheet on the previous page, complete the special gifts profile on the following page. For each gift, count the number of boxes you have marked under it. (The marked boxes are all of your YES answers to questions). Make a line on the PROFILE at the appropriate number.

Here Is An Example: Here is how the person's score sheet was marked:

GENERAL QUALIFICATIONS
( ) #1
(X) #6
( ) #11
( ) #16
(X) #21
(X) #26
(X) #31
( ) #36
( ) #41
( ) #46

PROPHET (Preacher)
( ) #3
( ) #8
( ) #13
(X) #18
( ) #23
( ) #28
(X) #33
( ) #38
(X) #43
(X) #48

APOSTLE
( ) #2
(X) #7
(X) #12
( ) #17
(X) #22
( ) #27
(X) #32
(X) #37
( ) #42
( ) #47

EVANGELIST
(X) #4
(X) #9
(X) #14
(X) #19
(X) #24
( ) #29
(X) #34
(X) #39
(X) #44
(X) #49

PASTOR TEACHER
(X) #5
( ) #10
( ) #15
(X) #20
( ) #25
( ) #30
( ) #35
( ) #40
( ) #45
( ) #50

Here is how they used their answers to complete the graph:

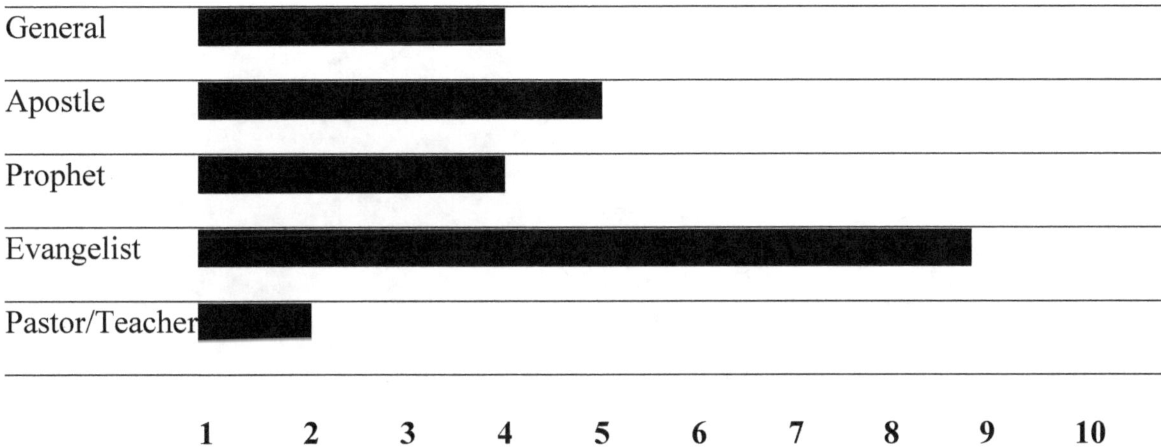

The long bars are the highest scores.
The short bars are the lowest scores.
Now, use your scoring sheet to complete your own special gifts profile:

SPECIAL GIFTS PROFILE

	1	2	3	4	5	6	7	8	9	10
General										
Apostle										
Prophet										
Evangelist										
Pastor/Teacher										

The long bars are your highest scores.

The short bars are your lowest scores.

SPIRITUAL GIFTS

SPIRITUAL GIFTS QUESTIONNAIRE:

YES	NO		
( )	( )	1.	Would you describe yourself as an effective public speaker?
( )	( )	2.	Do you find it easy and enjoyable to spend time in intense study and research of the Bible?
( )	( )	3.	Do you enjoy sharing the personal and emotional problems of people?
( )	( )	4.	Do you find yourself more concerned with how to apply God's Word than in simply trying to understand its message?
( )	( )	5.	Have you sensed that God has given you a special ability to learn and acquire knowledge concerning His Word?
( )	( )	6.	Do you enjoy motivating others to various tasks and ministries?
( )	( )	7.	Would other people describe you as a person who makes decisions easily?
( )	( )	8.	Do you seem to concentrate more on practical things that need to be done rather than on why they should be done?
( )	( )	9.	When you hear of someone who needs help, do you immediately offer your services?
( )	( )	10.	Would you rather give money to help than perform some manual task?
( )	( )	11.	Do you enjoy visiting people who are sick or disabled?
( )	( )	12.	Is your home the kind that most people feel comfortable in and will often drop by to visit with you unannounced?
( )	( )	13.	Do you find that you have the ability to believe things that other believers cannot seem to accept?
( )	( )	14.	Have other believers told you that you seem to always know whether something is right or wrong?
( )	( )	15.	When situations are not right, do you feel a burden to speak up in order to correct them?
( )	( )	16.	Do you like to prove and answer issues and questions?
( )	( )	17.	Have you found that people often ask you for advice about their personal problems?
( )	( )	18.	Do you find that you often know immediately what to do in a situation where others do not know what should be done?
( )	( )	19.	Do you find that people often come to you with difficult problems and questions from the Bible, seeking your understanding?
( )	( )	20.	Do you find yourself setting goals and objectives for yourself and your ministry as a believer?

YES	NO		
( )	( )	21.	Do you sense a great deal of responsibility to make decisions in behalf of others?
( )	( )	22.	Do you usually have a great deal of joy in doing things that need to be done no matter how small the task?
( )	( )	23.	Do you sense a special ministry to help others to become more effective in their work?
( )	( )	24.	When you hear of someone in need, do you immediately think of sending them some money?
( )	( )	25.	When you hear of someone in the hospital, does it challenge you to bring them some encouragement and cheer?
( )	( )	26.	Do you feel something is really missing in your life when you cannot have guests into your home?
( )	( )	27.	When people say something cannot be done or is impossible, do you feel the burden to believe God for it?
( )	( )	28.	Do you seem to have an understanding of people even though you do not know them well?
( )	( )	29.	Do you have a tendency to speak up when issues are being dealt with in a group, rather than remain silent and listen?
( )	( )	30.	When you hear a question or problem, are you anxious to both find and give an answer?
( )	( )	31.	Would you rather talk personally with someone about their problems rather than send them to someone else for help?
( )	( )	32.	Do people often seek your advice in difficult situations as to what you would do?
( )	( )	33.	In your study of God's Word have you observed that new insights and understanding of difficult subjects seem to come easy to you?
( )	( )	34.	When someone is not doing a job well, do you feel concern to help him become more effective in what he is doing?
( )	( )	35.	Do you sense a moral responsibility when giving direction and guidance, always thinking of how this will affect others?
( )	( )	36.	Do you have more satisfaction in doing a task than in what others thought of what you did?
( )	( )	37.	Do you see yourself more in a supportive ministry to others than in a place of leadership?
( )	( )	38.	Do you find yourself looking for opportunities to give your money without hearing appeals?
( )	( )	39.	Do you find it easy to express joy in the presence of those who are suffering physically?
( )	( )	40.	Do you love to entertain people in your home regardless of how well you know them?

YES NO

YES	NO		
)	( )	41.	Do you usually feel opposed to anyone who says that something cannot be done or accomplished?
( )	( )	42.	Do you sense often that what is being said is produced by the Devil rather than God, and has your judgment proven to be correct?
( )	( )	43.	Have you sensed that people feel conviction about wrong practices or doctrinal error when you share with them what the Bible says?
( )	( )	44.	Have people often said that you have an ability to explain difficult problems to them?
( )	( )	45.	Do you get joy out of encouraging people who are going through personal problems and trials?
( )	( )	46.	Do you find that people usually ask what you think about a situation with the belief that you will always know what to do?
( )	( )	47.	Have you noticed that you have the ability to understand difficult teachings of God's Word without a lot of research and study?
( )	( )	48.	Would you rather show someone else how to do a task than do it yourself?
( )	( )	49.	Do you enjoy giving direction to others and making decisions for them?
( )	( )	50.	Is it true that when you are asked to do a particular task you usually feel no pressure or obligation?
( )	( )	51.	Do you feel a special burden to relieve others of their duties in order to free them to do more important work?
( )	( )	52.	Do you find yourself responding immediately to financial needs by giving your money without a great deal of planning to do so?
( )	( )	53.	Is it easy for you to talk with those who are suffering physically?
( )	( )	54.	Do you consider your home as a real place of ministry to others?
( )	( )	55.	Have you discovered that you do not have to wait for clear evidence and direction before you make decisions?
( )	( )	56.	Do you find that you often evaluate people and the things they say as to whether it is right or wrong?
( )	( )	57.	When you speak God's Word do you usually think of how this is going to challenge and motivate those to whom you are speaking?
( )	( )	58.	Have people expressed to you how much they appreciate the way you explain things from the Bible?
( )	( )	59.	Do you find it easy to deal with people who are depressed or discouraged, experiencing joy in what can be accomplished?
( )	( )	60.	Have other believers referred to decisions you have made or advice you have given as being the right thing to do and the best for everyone?

YES NO

( ) ( ) 61. Do you seem to understand things about God's Word that other believers with the same background don't seem to know?

( ) ( ) 62. Do you have a special concern to train and disciple other believers to become leaders?

( ) ( ) 63. Do you find yourself constantly thinking of decisions that need to be made to provide direction to a group or organization?

( ) ( ) 64. Would you rather do a job yourself than work with a group in trying to accomplish it?

( ) ( ) 65. Do you believe that you would help almost anyone who had a need, if it was possible for you to do so?

( ) ( ) 66. Do you sense a great deal of joy in giving, regardless of the response of the one to whom you gave?

( ) ( ) 67. Do you often think of ways to help those who are suffering physically?

( ) ( ) 68. Would you like to have a regular ministry of entertaining people in your home regardless of who they are?

( ) ( ) 69. Can you believe for something when everyone else around you is disbelieving?

( ) ( ) 70. Do you feel a great responsibility toward God when you sense something is not right even if other believers do not seem to understand?

( ) ( ) 71. Have other believers shared with you that you have the ability to share God's Word with great effectiveness?

( ) ( ) 72. Do people come to you often, seeking answers to specific questions or problems?

( ) ( ) 73. Do you sense a great deal of love and compassion for people having personal and emotional problems?

( ) ( ) 74. When you give your advice to someone, do you emphasize more "how" it should be done, rather than "why" it should be done?

( ) ( ) 75. Have other believers frequently said that you have an ability to know and understand things of God's Word?

( ) ( ) 76. Do you have a special concern for helping people reach their goals and objectives?

( ) ( ) 77. Do people seem to depend upon you to make the major decisions for the group or the organization?

( ) ( ) 78. When you hear of a specific job that needs to be done, are you anxious to do it yourself?

( ) ( ) 79. Are you satisfied more with how a person has been helped by what you did, than by simply doing it?

( ) ( ) 80. When you give money, do you usually avoid letting others know what you did?

YES	NO		
( )	( )	81.	Would you enjoy a regular ministry to those who are suffering physically?
( )	( )	82.	Do you look at having people into your home as an exciting ministry more than an obligation?
( )	( )	83.	Have other believers often shared with you that you seem to have the ability to trust God in difficult situations?
( )	( )	84.	Have people often asked your opinion of someone or something that has been said as to whether you thought it was right or wrong?
( )	( )	85.	Do you believe you are gifted in communicating to others?
( )	( )	86.	Would you rather explain the meaning of a word than simply quote a verse to someone?
( )	( )	87.	Do you usually desire to hear others share their personal problems rather than share yours with someone else?
( )	( )	88.	Do other believers seem to follow your advice in difficult situations?
( )	( )	89.	Have you found in studying God's Word that you seem to know what a passage is saying before other believers discover it, even through you are studying it at the same time?
( )	( )	90.	Do you usually take the leadership in a group where none exists?
( )	( )	91.	Do you usually feel morally responsible for the long-range effects of your decisions?
( )	( )	92.	Would you rather do a particular job than spend time talking with people about their problems and needs?
( )	( )	93.	When someone asks for your help, do you have great difficulty in saying "no" to that person?
( )	( )	94.	When you give money to someone, do you find that you do not expect any appreciation in return?
( )	( )	95.	Do you feel compassion upon those who are suffering physically that makes you want to help them in some way?
( )	( )	96.	Do you find you can easily have people into your home without being overly concerned about how it looks?
( )	( )	97.	Do you feel a burden to encourage people to trust God when you see them defeated and discouraged?
( )	( )	98.	Have you felt a special responsibility to protect the truth of God's Word by exposing that which is wrong and sinful?
( )	( )	99.	Would you rather speak God's Word to others without much explanation than take the time to explain every detail?
( )	( )	100.	Do you usually organize your thoughts in a systematic way?
( )	( )	101.	When you hear of some believer who has "sinned" or fallen away," are you anxious to try to help them?
( )	( )	102.	Have the decisions and advice you have given in difficult situations proven to be right in most cases?

YES	NO		
( )	( )	103.	Do you have a great desire to share with other believers the meaning of a difficult Bible passage?
( )	( )	104.	Do you sense a great deal of joy in a leadership position, rather than frustration and difficulty?
( )	( )	105.	Have you had experience in making decisions in behalf of a group or organization that would affect everyone?
( )	( )	106.	Do you enjoy doing things that need to be done without being asked to do them?
( )	( )	107.	Do you look for opportunities to help other people?
( )	( )	108.	Do you see the giving of money as a great spiritual ministry which you believe God has given you?
( )	( )	109.	Do you find that visiting those who are suffering physically brings you joy rather than depressing you.
( )	( )	110.	Have other believers often referred to your ability to have people in your home and to the way God has used you in this?
( )	( )	111.	Have you seen God do mighty things in your life that others said could not be done but which you believed He would do?
( )	( )	112.	Do you feel you are helping other believers when you discern something is wrong, and have they readily accepted your evaluation?
( )	( )	113.	When an opportunity is given you to speak to other believers, do you find you would rather share Bible verses than your personal experiences?
( )	( )	114.	Have other believers told you that you should have a regular teaching ministry and have you felt the same?
( )	( )	115.	Do you enjoy a person-to-person ministry more than ministering to a group?
( )	( )	116.	Have you sensed a special ability to know what to do when dealing with difficult problems and situations?
( )	( )	117.	When you see other believers confused and lacking understanding about some difficult teaching of the Bible, have you sensed a responsibility to speak to them about what it means?
( )	( )	118.	Do you seem to know how to meet people's needs, goals, and desires without too much study and planning?
( )	( )	119.	Do you enjoy being the one with the overall responsibility for the direction and success of a group or organization?
( )	( )	120.	Do you find that it is not necessary for you to have a "job description" when you are asked to do a particular task?
( )	( )	121.	Have people often expressed that you have helped them by doing a particular job, relieving them of that responsibility so they could do something else?

YES NO

( ) ( ) 122. Are you really excited when someone asks you to help financially in some worthwhile project, seeing this as a great honor and privilege?

( ) ( ) 123. Are you willing and eager to spend time, money, and resources in order to help those who are suffering physically?

( ) ( ) 124. Do you find great joy in having people into your home rather than sensing that it is a responsibility that entails too much work?

( ) ( ) 125. Have you discovered an effective prayer ministry in your life with many wonderful answers to prayer that from a human point of view seem impossible or unlikely?

( ) ( ) 126. Have you often evaluated someone or something that was said that others did not see but which proved to be correct?

SPIRITUAL GIFTS SCORING SHEET:

When you have finished the questionnaire, complete the next page. As you did on the Special Gifts Scoring Sheet, for each question marked YES on the questionnaire, make a mark in the box by that question number. Do not make any marks for no answers.

PROPHECY	WORD OF WISDOM	ADMINISTRATION	GIVING	FAITH
( ) #1	( ) #4	( ) #7	( ) #10	( ) #13
( ) #15	( ) #18	( ) #21	( ) #24	( ) #27
( ) #29	( ) #32	( ) #35	( ) #38	( ) #41
( ) #43	( ) #46	( ) #49	( ) #52	( ) #55
( ) #57	( ) #60	( ) #63	( ) #66	( ) #69
( ) #71	( ) #74	( ) #77	( ) #80	( ) #83
( ) #85	( ) #88	( ) #91	( ) #94	( ) #97
( ) #99	( ) #102	( ) #105	( ) #108	( ) #111
( ) #113	( ) #116	( ) #119	( ) #122	( ) #125

TEACHING	WORD OF KNOWLEDGE	SERVING	SHOWING MERCY	DISCERNMENT
( ) #2	( ) #5	( ) #8	( ) #11	( ) #14
( ) #16	( ) #19	( ) #22	( ) #25	( ) #28
( ) #30	( ) #33	( ) #36	( ) #39	( ) #42
( ) #44	( ) #47	( ) #50	( ) #53	( ) #56
( ) #58	( ) #61	( ) #64	( ) #67	( ) #70
( ) #72	( ) #75	( ) #78	( ) #81	( ) #84
( ) #86	( ) #89	( ) #92	( ) #95	( ) #98
( ) #100	( ) #103	( ) #106	( ) #109	( ) #112
( ) #114	( ) #117	( ) #120	( ) #123	( ) #126

EXHORTATION	LEADERSHIP	HELPS	HOSPITALITY
( ) #3	( ) #6	( ) #9	( ) #12
( ) #17	( ) #20	( ) #23	( ) #26
( ) #31	( ) #34	( ) #37	( ) #40
( ) #45	( ) #48	( ) #51	( ) #54
( ) #59	( ) #62	( ) #65	( ) #68
( ) #73	( ) #76	( ) #79	( ) #82
( ) #87	( ) #90	( ) #93	( ) #96
( ) #101	( ) #104	( ) #107	( ) #110
() #115	( ) #118	( ) #121	( ) #124

SPIRITUAL GIFTS PROFILE:

Using the scoring sheet on the previous page, complete the special gifts profile on the following page.

For each gift, count the number of boxes you have marked under it. (The marked boxes are all of your YES answers to questions). Make a line on the PROFILE at the appropriate number.

After you have counted the boxes marked under each gift heading and marked it on the PROFILE, complete the PROFILE by filling in the lines to make a graph, just as you did on the Special Gifts Profile.

Gift										
Prophecy										
Teaching										
Exhortation										
Word of Wisdom										
Word of Knowledge										
Leadership										
Administration										
Serving										
Helps										
Giving										
Showing Mercy										
Hospitality										
Faith										
Discernment										
	1	2	3	4	5	6	7	8	9	10

The long bars are your highest scores.

The short bars are your lowest scores. The sign gifts are not included in this questionnaire because if you have these gifts you will know by the "signs" themselves.

CHAPTER ELEVEN

THE FRUIT OF THE HOLY SPIRIT

OBJECTIVES:

Upon completion of this chapter you will be able to:

- Identify the outer fruit of the Holy Spirit.
- Identify the inner fruit of the Holy Spirit.
- Explain the importance of the fruit of the Holy Spirit.
- Identify a Scripture reference which reveals we are chosen to bear fruit.
- Define the various inner fruit of the Spirit.
- Distinguish between peace of God and peace with God.

KEY VERSES:

> **But the fruit of the Spirit is love, joy, peace, longsuffering, gentleness, goodness faith,**
>
> **Meekness, temperance: against such there is no law. (Galatians 5:22-23)**

INTRODUCTION

This chapter discusses the fruit of the Holy Spirit. In the next chapter you will learn of contrasting qualities called the works of the flesh. In a final chapter you will learn how to develop spiritual fruit.

WHAT IS THE FRUIT?

The fruit of the Holy Spirit refers to the nature of the Spirit revealed in the life of the believer. It is spiritual qualities which should be evident in the lives of all Christians.

The gifts of the Holy Spirit are for power. The fruit of the Holy Spirit is for character in the life of a believer. The following chart illustrates differences between spiritual gifts and fruit:

Gifts	Fruit
-For ministry to the body -No believer has all -For power	-For maturity of the individual -Each believer should have all -For character

Spiritual fruit is evidence of spiritual maturity. Like fruit in the natural world, it is a product which is the result of the process of life. Spiritual fruit is Christian character in both personal and social conduct and is a product of the Holy Spirit at work in your life and your response to this work. Just as fruit takes time to develop in the natural world, spiritual fruit takes time to develop. It is the product of natural growth in the life of the Spirit.

TWO KINDS OF FRUIT

The Bible speaks of two kinds of spiritual fruit:

1. The fruit of evangelism.
2. The fruit of Godly spiritual qualities.

The Holy Spirit helps believers bear outer fruit by making them a powerful witness of the Gospel message. He also develops the inner fruit of Christ-like spiritual qualities in their lives.

OUTER FRUIT: EVANGELISM

NATURAL REPRODUCTION:

When Adam and Eve were created by God, the first command He gave them was to be "fruitful" and multiply in the natural world:

> **And God blessed them, and God said unto them, Be fruitful, and multiply, and replenish the earth and subdue it... (Genesis 1:28)**

In the natural world, God set a cycle of continuous reproduction:

> **While the earth remaineth, seedtime and harvest, and cold and heat, and summer and winter, and day and night shall not cease. (Genesis 8:22)**

SPIRITUAL REPRODUCTION:

From the beginning of the world, God called His people to spiritual reproduction as well as natural. Adam and Eve were to reproduce both spiritually and physically. God's original plan was that they were to fill the earth with people created in the image of God who walked in fellowship with God.

When God raised up the nation of Israel as a people through whom He could demonstrate His power and plan for the world, He called them to be spiritually reproductive:

> **Thou hast brought a vine out of Egypt: thou hast cast out the heathen, and planted it.**
>
> **Thou preparedest room before it, and didst cause it to take deep root, and it filled the land.**
>
> **The hills were covered with the shadow of it, and the boughs thereof were like the goodly cedars. (Psalms 80:8-10)**

The "vine" which God brought out of Egypt was the nation of Israel. He wanted them to bear spiritual fruit by revealing the true God to the heathen nations around them. Instead, Israel became like the heathen. They began to worship idols and wanted a visible human king to reign over them instead of the invisible King of Kings. Finally, God said of Israel:

> **Israel is an empty vine... (Hosea 10:1)**

Because of their spiritual unfruitfulness, Jesus said:

> **Therefore say I unto you, The kingdom of God shall be taken from you and given to a nation bringing forth the fruits thereof. (Matthew 21:43)**

Because of Israel's refusal to bear fruit, the Gospel of the Kingdom was extended to the Gentile nations. From the Gentiles God raised up the church to fulfill His plan of spiritual reproduction throughout the world.

CHOSEN TO BEAR FRUIT:

As believers, Jesus has chosen us to bear fruit through evangelism of the world:

> **Ye have not chosen me, but I have chosen you, and ordained you, that ye should go and bring forth fruit, and that your fruit should remain... (John 15:16)**

His last command to His followers was one of spiritual reproduction:

> **Go ye into all the world and preach the Gospel to every creature. (Mark 16:15)**

He challenged His disciples with a great vision of spiritual harvest:

> **Say not ye, There are yet four months, and then cometh harvest? behold, I say unto you, Lift up your eyes, and look on the fields; for they are white already to harvest.**
>
> **And he that reapeth receiveth wages, and gathereth fruit unto life eternal: that both he that soweth and he that reapeth may rejoice together. (John 4:35-36)**

Solomon said:

> **The fruit of the righteous is a tree of life; and he that winneth souls is wise. (Proverbs 11:30)**

The power of the Holy Spirit enables believers to be spiritually fruitful through evangelism:

> **But ye shall receive power after that the Holy Ghost is come upon you: and ye shall be witnesses unto me both in Jerusalem, and in all Judaea, and in Samaria, and unto the uttermost part of the earth. (Acts 1:8)**

The method of spiritual reproduction is given in II Timothy 2:2:

> **And the thing that thou hast heard of me among many witnesses, the same commit thou to faithful men, who shall be able to teach others also. (II Timothy 2:2)**

Just as God established a cycle of harvest in the natural world, He established a cycle of reproduction in the spiritual world. Each believer is to teach the Gospel to people who also reproduce by teaching others. Just as the natural cycle of seedtime and harvest is unending, so is the cycle of spiritual harvest.

(Because of the importance of the outer fruit of evangelism, Harvestime International Institute offers separate courses on this subject. Write for information on *"Strategies For Spiritual Harvest," "Methodologies of Multiplication,"* and *"Leaven-Like Evangelism"*).

INNER FRUIT: CHRIST-LIKENESS

In addition to the outer fruit of evangelism the Bible speaks of positive spiritual qualities produced in the life of a believer by the Holy Spirit. We call this fruit the inner fruit of Christ-likeness. This fruit is listed in Galatians 5:22-23:

> **But the fruit of the Spirit is love, joy, peace, longsuffering, gentleness, goodness faith,**
>
> **Meekness, temperance: against such there is no law. (Galatians 5:22-23)**

These are inner qualities the Holy Spirit wants to develop in the life of the believer. They are qualities that are like the spiritual qualities which were evident in the life of Jesus Christ. This is why we call them Christ-like qualities.

The word "fruit" is singular. It is not plural [fruits]. Remember that spiritual gifts are many and are divided among believers according to the will of the Holy Spirit. Fruit is singular. It can be understood by the natural example of grapes. A cluster of grapes has several individual grapes on it, but it is one cluster. In the natural world when grapes are picked from the vine they are picked in a cluster. This cluster of several grapes is called the "fruit" [singular] of the vine.

In the spiritual world the fruit of the Holy Spirit is similar to a cluster of grapes. It is separate spiritual qualities joined together in one cluster or fruit. This one fruit is spiritual maturity which is revealed in many Christ-like qualities.

One Fruit ___________	⇨	**Spiritual Maturity**
Many Qualities________	⇨	Meekness-Temperance Love-Joy-Peace Kindness-Goodness Longsuffering Faithfulness

God wants all believers to have the fruit of the Spirit. Unlike gifts which are plural [many] and are divided among believers, fruit [singular] is to be possessed by every believer.

The fruit of the Holy Spirit is found in every act of goodness, righteousness, and truth done by believers:

For the fruit of the Spirit is in all goodness and righteousness and truth. (Ephesians 5:9)

The following are the fruit of the Holy Spirit:

LOVE

Love is an emotion of deep affection, care, and concern. It is an unconditional giving of self to others regardless of their condition or circumstances. As you learned in your study of spiritual gifts, love is the key to operation of all spiritual gifts. It is also the quality from which all spiritual fruit develops. This is revealed when you compare the passage on the fruit of the Spirit in Galatians to the "love passage" in I Corinthians 13:

I Corinthians 13:1-7	**Galatians 5:22-23**
Does not seek her own, is not selfish or self-centered.	Love
Love does not rejoice in iniquity but rather rejoices in the truth.	Joy
Love is not easily provoked, but is serene and stable.	Peace
Love suffers long, perseveres, is patient.	Longsuffering
Love is merciful, thoughtful, and concerned; it envies not.	Kind [Gentleness]
Love is great, gracious, and generous; it is kind and good.	Goodness
Love thinks no evil, but has faith in God and others.	Faithfulness
Love is humble and gentle, does not vaunt itself.	Meekness
Love is disciplined and controlled, does not behave itself unbecomingly.	Temperance

Faith, which is both a gift and fruit of the Spirit, works by love:

> **...but faith which worketh by love. (Galatians 5:6)**

The spiritual fruit of love is not love as it is often depicted by the world. It is a love that is "unfeigned." This means it is a holy love. Unfeigned love is the type of love you are to show to others:

> **Seeing ye have purified your souls in obeying the truth through the Spirit unto unfeigned love of the brethren, see that ye love one another with a pure heart fervently. (I Peter 1:22)**

You are to love God:

> **And thou shalt love the Lord thy God with all thy heart, and with all thy soul, and with all thy mind, and with all thy strength: this if the first commandment. (Mark 12:30)**
>
> **(See also I John 2:5,15; 3:11-17; 4:7-20; 5:2; II John 1:5-6; Deuteronomy 6:5; Luke 10:27).**

You are to love your enemies:

> **But I say unto you which hear, Love your enemies, do good to them which hate you,**
>
> **Bless them that curse you, and pray for them which despitefully use you...**
>
> **And if ye do good to them which do good to you, what thank have ye? For sinners also do even the same...**
>
> **But love ye your enemies, and do good... (Luke 6:27,32,35)**
>
> **Ye have heard that it hath been said, Thou shalt love thy neighbor, and hate thine enemy.**
>
> **But I say unto you, Love your enemies, bless them that curse you, do good to them that hate you, and pray for them which despitefully use you, and persecute you. (Matthew 5:43-44)**

You are to love your neighbors as much as you love yourself:

> **...Thou shalt love thy neighbor as thyself. (Matthew 19:19)**

Jesus wants you to love others as much as He loved you:

A new commandment I give unto you, That ye love one another; as I have loved you, that ye also love one another. (John 13:34)

As the Father hath loved me, so have I loved you: continue ye in my love...

This is my commandment, That ye love one another as I have loved you. (John 15:9,12)

And I have declared unto them thy name, and will declare it; that the love wherewith thou hast loved me may be in them, and I in them. (John 17:26)

It is by our love for one another that we will be recognized as Christians:

By this shall all men know that ye are my disciples, if ye have love one to another. (John 13:35)

If you do not love other believers God's love is not in you:

He that saith he is in the light, and hateth his brother, is in darkness even until now.

He that loveth his brother abideth in the light, and there is none occasion of stumbling in him. (I John 2:9-10)

(This is a very important truth. Study it further in John 13:34; 14:15,21,23,31; 15:9-19; 17:26; 21:15-17).

Your love is to abound [to increase]:

And this I pray, that your love may abound yet more and more in knowledge and in all judgment. (Philippians 1:9)

And the Lord make you to increase and abound in love one toward another, and toward all men...(I Thessalonians 3:12)

You are to be rooted and grounded in love:

That Christ may dwell in your hearts by faith; that ye, being rooted and grounded in love,

May be able to comprehend with all saints what is the breadth, and length, and depth and height;

And to know the love of Christ which passeth knowledge, that ye might be filled with all the fullness of God. (Ephesians 3:17-19)

You are to "forbear" or relate to others in love:

With all lowliness and meekness, with longsuffering, forbearing one another in love. (Ephesians 4:2)

You are to keep yourself in love:

Keep yourselves in the love of God... (Jude 21)

...follow after righteousness, godliness, faith, love, patience, meekness. (I Timothy 6:11)

Your work for the Lord is to be a labor of love:

Remembering without ceasing your work of faith and labour of love... (I Thessalonians 1:3)

For God is not unrighteous to forget your work and labour of love, which ye have shewed toward His name, in that ye have ministered to the saints, and do minister. (Hebrews 6:10)

As we near the end of time here on earth, the love of many will not endure. It will "wax cold." This means people will become uncaring:

And because iniquity shall abound, the love of many shall wax cold. (Matthew 24:12)

But we are given the assurance that nothing can separate us from God's love:

Who shall separate us from the love of Christ? shall tribulation, or distress, or persecution, or famine, or nakedness, or peril, or sword?...

For I am persuaded, that neither death, nor life, nor angels, nor principalities, nor powers, nor things present, nor things to come,

Nor height, nor depth, nor any other creature, shall be able to separate us from the love of God, which is in Christ Jesus our Lord. (Romans 8:35,38-39)

David wrote much about love. See Psalms 31:23; 18:1; 40:16; 97:10; 116:1; 119:97, 113, 119, 127, 132, 159, 163, 105, 167; 122:6; 145:20. Study the book of I John. One of the major themes of this book is love.

JOY

Joy is a quality of gladness, delight, and jubilance.

The spiritual fruit of joy and the emotion of happiness are not the same. Each springs from a different source. Happiness comes from the world around you and is dependent upon your circumstances. Joy originates with the Spirit of God and is not dependent upon outward circumstances.

Jesus Christ brought joy at His birth:

And the angel said unto them, Fear not: for, behold, I bring you good tidings of great joy, which shall be to all people.

For unto you is born this day in the city of David a Saviour, which is Christ the Lord. (Luke 2:10-11)

It is God's desire that you have joy:

These things have I spoken unto you, that my joy might remain in you, and that your joy might be full. (John 15:11)

And now come I to thee; and these things I speak in the world, that they might have my joy fulfilled in themselves. (John 17:13)

The disciples were filled with joy and the Holy Ghost:

And the disciples were filled with joy, and with the Holy Ghost. (Acts 13:52)

The believer's source of joy is not worldly things but God:

...in thy presence, is fullness of joy; at thy right hand there are pleasures for evermore. (Psalms 16:11)

Because your joy is spiritual and not dependent on outward circumstances you can rejoice in temptation:

> **My brethren, count it all joy when ye fall into divers temptations... (James 1:2)**

You can also rejoice in tribulation [difficult times]:

> **...I am exceedingly joyful in all our tribulation. (II Corinthians 7:4)**

You can be longsuffering with joy:

> **...longsuffering with joyfulness. (Colossians 1:11)**

Joy is part of the Kingdom of God:

> **For the kingdom of God is not meat and drink; but righteousness, and peace, and joy in the Holy Ghost. (Romans 14:17)**

The Bible encourages believers to be joyful and express this joy unto the Lord:

> **But let all those that put their trust in thee rejoice: let them ever shout for joy....let them also that love thy name be joyful in thee. (Psalms 5:11)**

(See also Psalms 35:9; 63:5; 66:1; 81:1; 95:1-2; 149:5; 98:4,6,8; 100:1).

PEACE

Peace is a condition of quiet, calm, tranquility, and harmony. It is the absence of strife, anxiety, and concern. It is not just passivity. Maintaining peace for powerful action on the part of the peacemaker.

Confusion is the opposite of peace. God does not cause confusion. His desire is to bring peace:

> **For God is not the author of confusion, but of peace, as in all churches of the saints. (I Corinthians 14:33)**

Jesus brought peace to earth:

> **Glory to God in the highest, and on earth peace, good will toward men. (Luke 2:14)**

All true peace comes through Jesus Christ:

> **...preaching peace by Jesus Christ...(Acts 10:36)**

> **For He is our peace, who hath made both one, and hath broken down the middle wall of partition between us... (Ephesians 2:14)**

> **Therefore being justified by faith we have peace with God through our Lord Jesus Christ. (Romans 5:1)**

Jesus left His followers with a special peace:

> **Peace I leave with you, my peace I give unto you; not as the world giveth give I unto you. Let not your heart be troubled, neither let it be afraid. (John 14:27)**

The teachings of Jesus brought peace:

> **These things have I spoken to you that in me ye might have peace. (John 16:33)**

The Gospel is a message of peace:

> **And your feet shod with the preparation of the gospel of peace. (Ephesians 6:15)**

There are two types of peace. The first is peace with God:

> **Therefore being justified by faith, we have peace with God through our Lord Jesus Christ. (Romans 5:1)**

After you have made peace with God, you can have the peace of God in your life:

> **And the peace of God which passeth all understanding, shall keep your hearts and minds through Christ Jesus. (Philippians 4:7)**

We are told to follow after things which result in peace:

> **Let us therefore follow after the things which make for peace, and things wherewith one may edify another. (Romans 14:19)**

We are to live in peace:

...be perfect, be of good comfort, be of one mind, live in peace; and the God of love and peace shall be with you. (II Corinthians 13:11)

We are to live peaceably with all men:

Follow peace with all men... (Hebrews 12:14)

We are to keep the unity of the Spirit through peace:

Endeavoring to keep the unity of the Spirit in the bond of peace. (Ephesians 4:3)

The peace of God is to rule in our hearts:

And let the peace of God rule in your hearts, to the which also ye are called in one body... (Colossians 3:15)

We are to be found in peace at all times:

...that ye may be found of Him in peace... (II Peter 3:14)

LONGSUFFERING

Longsuffering is the quality of patience. It is the ability to cheerfully bear an unbearable situation and patiently endure. Longsuffering is a quality of God:

...The Lord God, merciful and gracious, longsuffering and abundant in goodness and truth. (Exodus 34:6)

The Lord is longsuffering, and of great mercy, forgiving iniquity and transgression... (Numbers 14:18)

But thou, O Lord, art a God full of compassion, and gracious, longsuffering, and plenteous in mercy and truth. (Psalms 86:15)

The Lord is not slack concerning His promise, as some men count slackness; but is longsuffering to us-ward, not willing that any should perish, but that all should come to repentance.

And account that the longsuffering of our Lord is salvation... (II Peter 3:15)

Or despisest thou the riches of His goodness and forbearance and longsuffering... (Romans 2:4)

Longsuffering was a quality evident in the ministry of the Apostle Paul:

But thou hast fully known my doctrine, manner of life, purpose, faith, longsuffering, charity, patience... (II Timothy 3:10)

We are told to be longsuffering with joyfulness:

Strengthened with all might, according to His glorious power, unto all patience, and longsuffering with joyfulness. (Colossians 1:11)

We are called to be longsuffering:

With all lowliness and meekness, with longsuffering, forbearing one another in love. (Ephesians 4:2)

We are to preach the Word of God with longsuffering:

Preach the word; be instant in season, out of season; reprove, rebuke, exhort with all longsuffering and doctrine. (II Timothy 4:2)

Believers are to "put on" longsuffering as a spiritual quality:

Put on therefore, as the elect of God, holy and beloved, bowels of mercies, kindness, humbleness of mind, meekness, longsuffering. (Colossians 3:12)

GENTLENESS

Gentleness is the quality of having a mild manner, not severe, violent, or loud. It is a quiet and respectful kindness.

The Bible warns believers not to strive but to be gentle to all men:

And the servant of the Lord must not strive; but be gentle unto all men, apt to teach, patient...(II Timothy 2:24)

We are not to be brawlers. Brawlers are people who are always fighting or arguing:

To speak evil of no man, to be no brawlers, but gentle, shewing all meekness unto all men. (Titus 3:2)

We are to be easily entreated. That means we are to be easily approached by others because of our gentle nature:

> **But the wisdom that is from above is first pure, then peaceable, gentle, and easy to be entreated, full of mercy and good fruits, without partiality, and without hypocrisy. (James 3:17)**

David wrote:

> **Thou hast also given me the shield of thy salvation; and thy right hand hath holden me up, and thy gentleness hath made me great. (Psalms 18:35)**

GOODNESS

Goodness is acts of holiness or righteousness. Goodness is a quality of God:

> **..the goodness of God endureth continually. (Psalms 52:1)**

> **Oh that men would praise the Lord for his goodness and for His wonderful works to the children of men. (Psalms 107:8,15,21,31)**

> **My goodness, and my fortress; my high tower, and my deliverer; my shield, and He in whom I trust; who subdueth my people under me. (Psalms 144:2)**

The earth shows the goodness of God:

> **...the earth is full of the goodness of the Lord. (Psalms 33:5)**

God crowns the year with His goodness. This means all the blessings of each year are from Him:

> **Thou crownest the year with thy goodness... (Psalms) 65:11**

The goodness of God is shown to sinners to lead them to repentance:

> **Or despisest thou the riches of His goodness and forbearance and longsuffering; not knowing that the goodness of God leadeth thee to repentance? (Romans 2:4)**

King David said that he would have fainted had it not been for the goodness of God:

> **I had fainted, unless I had believed to see the goodness of the Lord in the land of the living. (Psalms 27:13)**

David said God's goodness is laid up for us:

> **Oh how great is thy goodness, which thou hast laid up for them that fear thee; which thou hast wrought for them that trust in thee before the sons of men. (Psalms 31:19)**

God fills the hungry with goodness:

> **For He satisfieth the longing soul, and filleth the hungry soul with goodness. (Psalms 107:9)**

As a believer, the goodness and mercy of God follows you:

> **Surely goodness and mercy shall follow me all the days of my life... (Psalms 23:6)**

FAITH

You learned about faith when you studied it as a spiritual gift. The concepts taught about faith as a gift are also applicable to faith as a fruit.

But remember the difference between the two which was explained previously. Faith as a gift is power. It is an action. It is a strong confidence in God which enables a believer to take action where others will not act because of unbelief. Faith as a fruit is character. It is an attitude of faith towards God. It is developed through the process of His life within us bringing spiritual growth. While everyone does not have the gift of faith, the fruit of faith should be evident in the lives of all believers.

MEEKNESS

Meekness is controlled strength. Meekness is to be the method used in restoring a backslider. A backslider is one who goes back into a life of sin after having received Jesus as Savior:

> **Put on therefore, as the elect of God, holy and beloved, bowels of mercies, kindness, humbleness of mind, meekness, longsuffering;**
>
> **Forbearing one another and forgiving one another, if any man have a quarrel against any: even as Christ forgave you, so also do ye. (Colossians 3:12-13)**

Brethren if a man be overtaken in a fault, ye which are spiritual, restore such an one in the spirit of meekness; considering thyself, lest thou also be tempted. (Galatians 6:1)

Meekness keeps unity in the church:

...walk worthy of the vocation wherewith ye are called,

With all lowliness and meekness, with longsuffering, forbearing one another in love;

Endeavoring to keep the unity of the Spirit in the bond of peace. (Ephesians 4:1-3)

Meekness should be used in dealing with all men:

And the servant of the Lord must not strive; but be gentle unto all men, apt to teach, patient,

In meekness instructing those that oppose themselves; if God peradventure will give them repentance to the acknowledging of the truth. (II Timothy 2:24-25)

To speak evil of no man, to be no brawlers, but gentle, shewing all meekness unto all men. (Titus 3:2)

You are to receive God's Word with meekness:

Wherefore lay apart all filthiness and superfluity of naughtiness, and receive with meekness the engrafted word, which is able to save your souls. (James 1:21)

A wise man is a meek man:

Who is a wise man and endued with knowledge among you? let him shew out of a good conversation his works with meekness of wisdom. (James 3:13)

Believers are encouraged to seek this quality of meekness:

Put on therefore, as the elect of god, holy and beloved, bowels of mercies kindness humbleness of mind, meekness, longsuffering. (Colossians 3:12)

But thou, O man of God, flee these things; and follow after righteousness, godliness, faith, love, patience, meekness. (I Timothy 6:11)

Seek ye the Lord, all ye meek of the earth, which have wrought His judgment; seek righteousness, seek meekness... (Zephaniah 2:3)

TEMPERANCE

Temperance is moderation in emotions, thoughts, and actions. It is self-control. Temperance is mastery in all things:

But I keep under my body and bring it into subjection: lest that by any means, when I have preached to others, I myself should be a castaway. (I Corinthians 9:27) (See I Corinthians 9:19-27).

We are told to add temperance to our lives:

And to knowledge temperance; and to temperance patience... (II Peter 1:6)

Temperance was part of Paul's message of the Gospel:

And he reasoned of righteousness, temperance, and judgment to come... (Acts 24:25)

IMPORTANCE OF THE FRUIT

Jesus placed great emphasis on fruit bearing. In one parable He said:

A certain man had a fig tree planted in his vineyard; and he came and sought fruit thereon, and found none.

Then said he unto the dresser of his vineyard, Behold these three years I come seeking fruit on this fig tree, and find none: cut it down: why cumbereth it the ground?

And he answering said unto him, Lord, let it alone this year also, till I shall dig about it, and dung it:

And if it bear fruit, well: and if not, then after that thou shalt cut it down. (Luke 13:6-9)

Another time Jesus saw a fig tree which had no fruit:

Now in the morning as He returned into the city, He hungered.

And when He saw a fig tree in the way, He came to it, and found nothing thereon, but leaves only, and said unto it, Let no fruit grow on thee henceforward for ever. (Matthew 21:18-19)

Jesus cursing the fig tree was not an act of anger because He was hungry and the tree had no fruit. He was teaching an important truth. The fig tree had a good appearance. It had green leaves and looked as if it should be fruitful. But it had no fruit.

Some people give the outward appearance of being spiritual, but inwardly they do not have the spiritual fruit of Christ-likeness. This was the condition of the Pharisees, a religious group at the time of Christ. Jesus said to them:

Woe unto you, scribes and Pharisees, hypocrites! for ye are like unto whited sepulchres, which indeed appear beautiful outward, but are within full of dead men's bones, and of all uncleanness. (Matthew 23:27)

God is concerned about fruitfulness rather than the appearance of fruitfulness.

Generally speaking, more emphasis has been placed on the gifts rather than the fruit of the Holy Spirit in modern ministry. But the Bible emphasizes spiritual fruit:

Wherefore by their fruits you shall know them... (Matthew 7:20)

The fruit, or spiritual qualities shown by a person, reveals what he is like inside:

For a good tree bringeth not forth corrupt fruit; neither doth a corrupt tree bring forth good fruit.

For every tree is known by his own fruit. For of thorns men do not gather figs, nor of a bramble bush gather they grapes.

A good man out of the good treasure of his heart bringeth forth that which is good; and an evil man out of the evil treasure of his heart bringeth forth that which is evil: for of the abundance of the heart his mouth speaketh. (Luke 6:43-45)

A man may have personal appeal [charisma] that can be mistaken for spiritual power. He may even do miracles in the name of the Lord. But Jesus said:

Not every one that saith unto me, Lord, Lord, shall enter into the kingdom of heaven; but he that doeth the will of my Father which is in heaven.

> **Many will say to me in that day, Lord, Lord, have we not prophesied in thy name? and in thy name have cast out devils? and in thy name done many wonderful works?**
>
> **And then will I profess unto them, I never knew you: depart from me, ye that work iniquity. (Matthew 7:21-23)**

Jude warned against those who would "creep in" to the church and teach false doctrine. He said one of the ways to recognize them was by the lack of fruit in their lives:

> **...These are...trees whose fruit withereth, without fruit, twice dead, plucked up by the roots. (Jude 12)**

The important thing in any ministry is the fruit because... "By their FRUITS ye shall know them" (Matthew 7:20).

In the natural world it is the fruit which carries within it the seeds which reproduce. In the spirit world it is the fruit of the Holy Spirit which has the capacity for spiritual reproduction:

-The fruit of Christ-like qualities in lives of believers draws sinful men to God.

-The fruit of evangelism spreads the Gospel of the Kingdom and results in spiritual harvest throughout the world.

SELF-TEST

1. What is the outer fruit of the Spirit?

____

2. What is the inner fruit of the Spirit?

____

3. List the qualities of the inner fruit of the Holy Spirit:

_______________ _______________

_______________ _______________

_______________ _______________

_______________ _______________

____

4. What Scripture reference reveals that Jesus has chosen us to bear fruit?

____

5. Write the Key Verses from memory.

____

____

____

____

6. Read the list of spiritual fruit of the Holy Spirit in list one. Read the definitions in list two. Write the number of the definition which describes the fruit on the blank provided.

List One	**List Two**
_____Temperance	1. Deep affection, care
_____Faith	2. Gladness, delight
_____Meekness	3. Quiet, calm, harmony
_____Gentleness	4. Patient endurance
_____Goodness	5. Mild manner, not severe
_____Joy	6. Righteous acts
_____Longsuffering	7. Strong confidence in God
_____Peace	8. Controlled strength
_____Love	9. Self-control

7. Why is the fruit of the Spirit important?

____

____

8. What is the difference between the peace of God and peace with God?

____

____

(Answers to tests are provided at the conclusion of the final chapter in this manual.)

FOR FURTHER STUDY

1. Read Matthew 5:1-12. How many inner fruit of Christ-likeness can you find in this passage? For example, the fruit of joy is mentioned in verse 12.

2. Read I Corinthians chapter 13 which concerns the spiritual fruit of love. How many other spiritual fruit can you see expressed in love? For example, "believes all things" in verse 7 is the fruit of faith.

3. The fruit of the Holy Spirit are manifestations of God's character. God is a God of:

Love:	I John 4:16; Titus 3:4
Joy:	Matthew 25:21
Peace:	Philippians 4:7
Longsuffering:	II Peter 3:9,15
Gentleness:	Matthew 11:28-30
Goodness:	II Peter 1:3
Faithfulness:	II Timothy 2:13
Meekness:	Zephaniah 2:3
Temperance:	Hebrews 12:11 (God's chastening demonstrates moderation).

4. Jesus Christ had all the fruit of the Holy Spirit evident in His life:

Outer Fruit: Evangelism: John 10:16; Mark 1:38

Inner Fruit:

Love:	Mark 10:21; John 11:5,36
Joy:	John 15:11
Peace:	John 14:27
Longsuffering:	I Peter 3:15
Gentleness:	II Corinthians 10:1
Goodness:	Romans 11:22
Faith:	Matthew 17:14-21
Meekness:	II Corinthians 10:1
Temperance:	Luke 4:1-13

Read the books of Matthew, Mark, Luke, and John. Add to this outline other references where Jesus demonstrated fruit of the Holy Spirit.

CHAPTER TWELVE

THE WORKS OF THE FLESH

OBJECTIVES:

Upon completion of this chapter you will be able to:

- Identify the works of the flesh.
- Explain how to walk in the Spirit rather than in the flesh.

KEY VERSES:

> **Now the works of the flesh are manifest, which are these: Adultery, fornication, uncleanness, lasciviousness,**
>
> **Idolatry, witchcraft, hatred, variance, emulations, wrath, strife, seditions, heresies,**
>
> **Envyings, murders, drunkenness, revellings, and such like; of the which I tell you before, as I have also told you in time past, that they which do such things shall not inherit the Kingdom of God. (Galatians 5:19-21)**

INTRODUCTION

This chapter concerns the works of the flesh, sinful qualities which contrast the fruit of the Holy Spirit.

WHAT ARE WORKS OF THE FLESH?

The works of the flesh are characteristics of the sinful nature of man caused by lust [sinful desire]. They are opposites of the qualities which the Holy Spirit wants to develop in your life.

A SPIRITUAL BATTLE

There is a constant spiritual battle going on in the life of a believer. The works of the flesh are trying to destroy the fruit of the Holy Spirit:

For the flesh lusteth against the Spirit, and the Spirit against the flesh: and these are contrary the one to the other: so that ye cannot do the things that ye would. (Galatians 5:17)

The fleshly desires of natural man are contrary to the nature of the Holy Spirit. The works of the flesh are:

...Adultery, fornication, uncleanness, lasciviousness,

Idolatry, witchcraft, hatred, variance, emulations, wrath, strife, seditions, heresies,

Envyings, murders, drunkenness, revellings, and such like... (Galatians 5:19-21)

Although the results of these sins are visible in wrong actions, the cause is not visible. The cause is sinful desires [lusts] of the heart:

And He saith unto them, Are ye so without understanding also? Do ye not perceive that whatsoever thing from without entereth into the man, it cannot defile him...

And He said, That which cometh out of the man, that defileth the man.

For from within, out of the heart of men, proceed evil thoughts, adulteries, fornications, murders,

Thefts, covetousness, wickedness, deceit, lasciviousness, an evil eye, blasphemy, pride, foolishness;

And these evil things come from within, and defile the man. (Mark 7:18,20-23)

The sins listed in Galatians 5:19-21 are not all of the sins identified in the Bible. They are a group of sins called "works of the flesh" which contrast the fruit of the Spirit. This is why we are studying these specific sins.

ADULTERY

Adultery is sexual intercourse by a married person with someone who is not their spouse. One of the first ten commandments from God was:

Thou shalt not commit adultery. (Exodus 20:14)

In Old Testament times when a person committed adultery he was put to death:

And the man that committeth adultery with another man's wife, even he that committeth adultery with his neighbour's wife, the adulterer and the adulteress shall surely be put to death. (Leviticus 20:10)

Both Jesus and Paul repeated the warning against adultery in the New Testament:

Thou knowest the commandments, Do not commit adultery... (Mark 10:19)

For this, Thou shalt not commit adultery... (Romans 13:9)

Jesus expanded the meaning of adultery to include evil sexual desires of the heart:

Ye have heard that it was said by them of old time, Thou shalt not commit adultery:

But I say unto you, That whosoever looketh on a woman to lust after her hath committed adultery with her already in his heart. (Matthew 5:27-28)

Adultery also includes divorcing a mate and remarrying without Biblical cause:

But I say unto you, That whosoever shall put away his wife, saving for the cause of fornication, causeth her to commit adultery; and whosoever shall marry her that is divorced committeth adultery. (Matthew 5:32)

And if a woman shall put away her husband, and be married to another, she committeth adultery. (Mark 10:12)

When a person commits adultery he is sinning against his own soul:

But whoso comitteth adultery with a woman lacketh understanding: he that doeth it destroyeth his own soul. (Proverbs 6:32)

God judges those who commit adultery:

Marriage is honourable in all, and the bed undefiled: but whoremongers and adulterers God will judge. (Hebrews 13:4)

Those who commit adultery do not inherit the Kingdom of God:

Know ye not that the unrighteous shall not inherit the kingdom of God? Be not deceived: neither fornicators, nor idolaters, nor adulterers, nor effeminate, nor abusers of themselves with mankind,

Nor thieves, nor covetous, nor drunkards nor revilers, nor extortioners, shall inherit the Kingdom of God. (I Corinthians 6:9)

One of the characteristics by which you can recognize false teachers is by the sin of adultery:

...there shall be false teachers among you...Having eyes full of adultery, and that cannot cease from sin... (II Peter 2:1,14)

The Bible warns:

...the adulteress will hunt for the precious life. (Proverbs 6:26)

FORNICATION

Fornication is sexual intercourse by two people who are not married to each other. This sin includes adultery which is sexual intercourse by a married person with someone who is not their mate. Fornication also includes sexual intercourse between people who are not married. It includes sexual deviation such as homosexuality [with someone of the same sex] and incest.

Fornication can be a Biblically permitted reason for divorce:

But I say unto you, That whosoever shall put away his wife, saving for the cause of fornication, causeth her to commit adultery: and whosoever shall marry her that is divorced commiteth adultery. (Matthew 5:32)

Fornicators will not inherit the Kingdom of God:

Know ye not that the unrighteous shall not inherit the kingdom of God? Be not deceived: neither fornicators..shall inherit the kingdom of God. (I Corinthians 6:9-10)

The Bible tells us to abstain [refrain] from fornication:

For this is the will of God, even your sanctification, that ye should abstain from fornication. (I Thessalonians 4:3)

Nevertheless to avoid fornication, let every man have his own wife, and let every woman have her own husband. (I Corinthians 7:2)

Neither let us commit fornication, as some of them committed... (I Corinthians 10:8)

The body is not intended for fornication because it belongs to the Lord. For this reason, you must flee fornication:

...Now the body is not for fornication, but for the Lord, and the Lord for the body...

Flee fornication. Every sin that a man doeth is without the body; but he that committeth fornication sinneth against his own body.

What? Know ye not that your body is the temple of the Holy Ghost which is in you which ye have of God, and ye are not your own?

For ye are bought with a price; therefore glorify God in your body, and in your spirit, which are God's. (I Corinthians 6:13,18-20)

It is your responsibility to mortify fornication:

Mortify therefore your members which are upon the earth...fornication... (Colossians 3:5)

Fornication is not to even be named among believers:

But fornication, and all uncleanness, or covetousness, let it not be once named among you, as becometh saints. (Ephesians 5:3)

If a person continues in fornication, he finally will be given over to it totally. According to Romans l, it can even lead to homosexuality. Eventually, his conscience will no longer be bothered by it:

For this cause God gave them up...Being filled with all unrighteousness, fornication...(Romans 1:26,29)

UNCLEANNESS

Uncleanness is the opposite of being clean. In this passage on the works of the flesh, the word "uncleanness" means being spiritually or morally unclean.

God does not want His people to be unclean:

But fornication, and all uncleanness, or covetousness, let it not be once named among you, as becometh saints. (Ephesians 5:2)

For God hath not called us unto uncleanness, but unto holiness. (I Thessalonians 4:7)

It is your responsibility to mortify uncleanness and discipline yourself to live a holy life:

Mortify therefore your members which are upon the earth: fornication, uncleanness, inordinate affection, evil concupiscence, and covetousness, which is idolatry. (Colossians 3:5)

Having therefore these promises, dearly beloved, let us cleanse ourselves from all filthiness of the flesh and spirit, perfecting holiness in the fear of God. (II Corinthians 7:1)

That every one of you should know how to possess his vessel in sanctification and honour... (I Thessalonians 4:4)

If you do not mortify uncleanness then you will yield to it:

I speak after the manner of men because of the infirmity of your flesh; for as ye have yielded your members servants to uncleanness and to iniquity unto iniquity; even so now yield your members servants to righteousness unto holiness. (Romans 6:19)

If you continue to yield to uncleanness you will eventually give yourself over to it:

Who being past feeling have given themselves over unto lasciviousness, to work all uncleanness with greediness.

But ye have not so learned Christ. (Ephesians 4:19-20)

If you continue to live in spiritual uncleanness [sin], God will give you over to it:

Wherefore God also gave them up to uncleanness through the lusts of their own hearts... (Romans 1:24)

When a man is given over by God to something, his conscience ceases to function and he is totally controlled by it. He will perish in his sin unless he repents:

But chiefly them that walk after the flesh in the lust of uncleanness...these as natural brute beasts, made to be taken and destroyed, speak evil of the things they understand not; and shall utterly perish in their own corruption... (II Peter 2:10,12)

Look at the following chart. You will note that when these verses on uncleanness are put together, a pattern emerges. You have the power to either mortify or yield to sin. If you mortify uncleanness, it will lead to holiness in your life. If you yield to it, you will eventually give yourself over to it. Finally, God will give you over to it and you will perish in your own corruption:

UNCLEANNESS: A PATTERN OF CHOICE

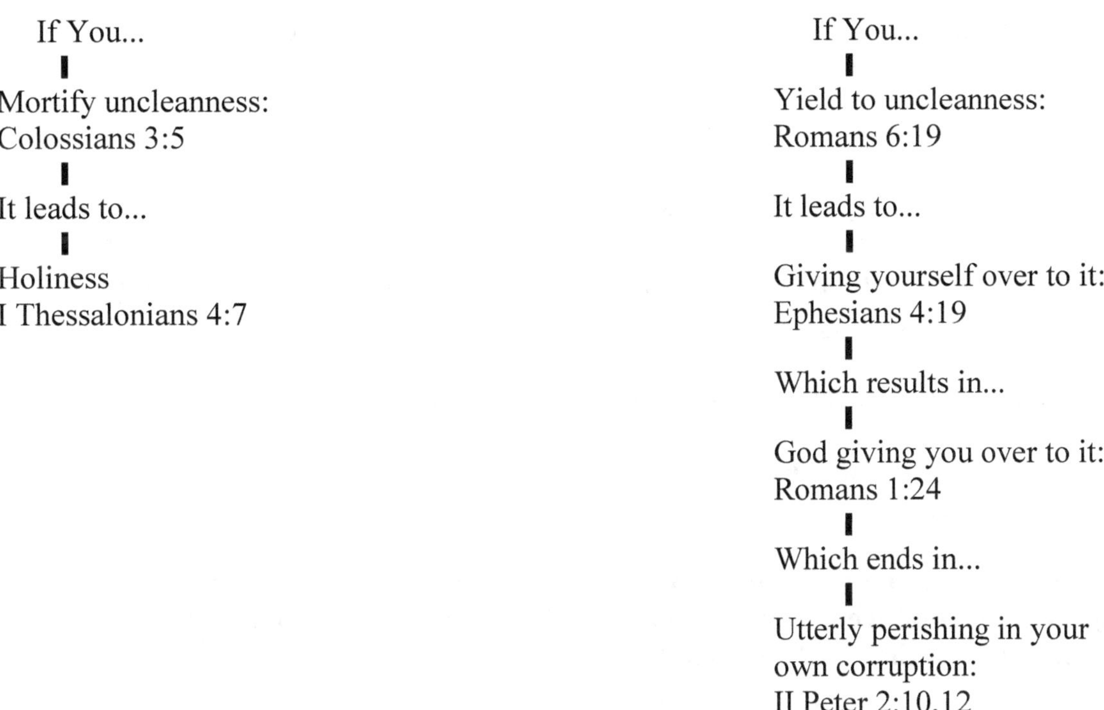

LASCIVIOUSNESS

Lasciviousness is the sin of lust, sinful emotions, and lewdness. It is filthy and shameless conduct. Lasciviousness is one of the characteristics by which you can recognize false teachers:

For there are certain men crept in unawares, who were before of old ordained to this condemnation, ungodly men, turning the grace of our God into lasciviousness, and denying the only Lord God, and our Lord Jesus Christ. (Jude 4)

In times past you may have been lascivious. As a believer, you are no longer to continue this behavior:

> **That he no longer should live the rest of his time in the flesh to the lusts of men, but to the will of God.**
>
> **For the time past of our life may suffice us to have wrought the will of the Gentiles, when we walked in lasciviousness, lusts, excess of wine, revellings, banquetings, and abominable idolatries... (I Peter 4:2-3)**

The Bible teaches that if you continue to be lascivious, you will eventually give yourself over to it without conscience:

> **Who being past feeling have given themselves over unto lasciviousness, to work uncleanness with greediness. (Ephesians 4:19)**

IDOLATRY

Idolatry is the worship of idols. This does not just mean the worship of images made out of stone, wood, or precious metals. An idol is anything that is more important to you than God. Idolaters are those who practice idolatry and worship something other than the true God. Idolatry is the lack of acknowledgment of the rightful position of God in your life.

One of the first commandments given by God concerned idolatry:

> **Turn ye not unto idols, nor make to yourselves molten gods: I am the Lord your God. (Leviticus 19:4)**
>
> **Ye shall make you no idols nor graven image, neither rear you up a standing image, neither shall ye set up any image of stone in your land, to bow down unto it: for I am the Lord your God. (Leviticus 26:1)**

The gods of heathen nations are called idols:

> **For all the gods of the nations are idols: but the Lord made the heavens. (Psalms 96:5)**

You will be confounded [or confused] if you serve idols:

> **Confounded be all they that serve graven images, that boast themselves of idols... (Psalms 97:7)**

The idols of the heathen are the work of man. They have no power or true spiritual significance:

The idols of the heathen are silver and gold, the work of men's hands. They have mouths, but they speak not; eyes have they, but they see not;

They have ears, but they hear not; neither is there any breath in their mouths.

They that make them are like unto them: so is every one that trusteth in them. (Psalms 135:15-18) (See also Psalms 115:4-8).

A Christian cannot worship idols:

And what agreement hath the temple of God with idols? (II Corinthians 6:16)

You are not to even keep company with idolaters:

But now I have written unto you not to keep company, if any man that is called a brother be a fornicator, or covetous, or an idolater, or a railer, or a drunkard, or an extortioner; with such an one go not to eat. (I Corinthians 5:11)

You are warned to keep yourself from idols:

Little children, keep yourselves from idols. (I John 5:21)

Idolaters will not be part of the Kingdom of God:

Know ye not that the unrighteous shall not inherit the kingdom of God? Be not deceived...neither idolaters...shall inherit the kingdom of God. (I Corinthians 6:9-10)

The Bible reveals the destination of idolaters:

But the fearful, and unbelieving, and the abominable and murderers, and whoremongers, and sorcerers, and idolaters, and all liars, shall have their part in the lake which burneth with fire and brimstone; which is the second death. (Revelation 21:8)

For without are dogs, and sorcerers, and whoremongers, and murderers, and idolaters, and whosoever loveth and maketh a lie. (Revelation 22:15)

The Bible calls covetousness a form of idolatry. Covetousness is wanting something with an intense and wrong desire. You are to mortify and destroy covetousness:

Mortify therefore your members which are upon the earth: fornication, uncleanness, inordinate affection, evil concupiscence, and covetousness, which is idolatry. (Colossians 3:5)

You may have been an idolater in times past, but believers are no longer to continue with this practice:

That he no longer should live the rest of his time in the flesh to the lusts of men, but to the will of God.

For the time past of our life may suffice us to have wrought the will of the Gentiles, when we walked in lasciviousness, lusts, excess of wine, revellings, banquetings, and abominable idolatries... (I Peter 4:2-3)

For they themselves shew of us what manner of entering in we had unto you, and how ye turned to God from idols to serve the living and true God. (I Thessalonians 1:9)

WITCHCRAFT

Witchcraft is the practice of witches including white and black magic, sorcery, astrology, voodoo, use of potions, spells, enchantments, and drugs. It includes all Satanic practices and worship.

The meaning of witchcraft can be expanded to include any control and manipulation of others. Even though you are not involved in Satanic witchcraft, you can be guilty of "witchcraft" as a sin of the flesh if you try to manipulate, control, or pray against others.

Witchcraft is spiritual rebellion against God. God says the sin of rebellion is as bad as witchcraft:

For rebellion is as the sin of witchcraft... (I Samuel 15:23)

HATRED

Hatred is the opposite of love. It is an emotion of intense dislike. It is evil feelings towards others. The Bible says that hatred stirs up strife:

Hatred stirreth up strife; but love covereth all sins. (Proverbs 10:12)

It is better to be where love is than with those who are filled with hatred:

Better is a dinner of herbs where love is, than a stalled ox and hatred therewith. (Proverbs 15:17)

Hatred covered by deceit will be revealed by God:

Whose hatred is covered by deceit, his wickedness shall be shewed before the whole congregation. (Proverbs 26:26)

Deceit here means pretending to like someone when in reality you hate them.

VARIANCE

Variance is disagreement, disharmony, and dissension. It is similar to strife. This word is used only one other place in the Bible; when Jesus speaks of "variance" in the family as a sign of the last days of time (Matthew 10:35).

EMULATIONS

Emulation is the desire to copy others and to equal or excel them. It is a spirit of rivalry and a form of jealousy. This passage in Galatians is the only reference in the Bible where the word is used in this manner (Galatians 5:19-21).

WRATH

Wrath is violent anger, an angry act, rage. The Bible says wrath is cruel:

Wrath is cruel, and anger is outrageous; but who is able to stand before envy. (Proverbs 27:4)

A man of great wrath will suffer because of it:

A man of great wrath shall suffer punishment; for if thou deliver him, yet thou must do it again. (Proverbs 19:19)

Wise men will turn away from wrath:

...Wise men turn away wrath. (Proverbs 29:8)

When you were an unbeliever you were a child of wrath:

Among whom also we all had our conversation in times past in the lusts of our flesh, fulfilling the desires of the flesh and of the mind; and were by nature the children of wrath, even as others. (Ephesians 2:3)

Now wrath should not operate in your life:

> **Let all bitterness, and wrath, and anger, and clamour, and evil speaking, be put away from you, with all malice... (Ephesians 4:31)**

You are to put off wrath:

> **But now ye also put off all these; anger, wrath, malice, blasphemy, filthy communication out of your mouth. (Colossians 3:8)**

You are to forsake wrath:

> **Cease from anger, and forsake wrath: fret not thyself in any wise to do evil. (Psalms 37:8)**

You are to be slow to wrath:

> **Wherefore, my beloved brethren, let every man be swift to hear, slow to speak, slow to wrath;**
>
> **For the wrath of man worketh not the righteousness of God. (James 1:19,20)**
>
> **He that is slow to wrath is of great understanding; but he that is hasty of spirit exalteth folly. (Proverbs 14:29)**

There is a relation between wrath and the next work of the flesh you will study which is strife. The Bible describes this relationship:

> **A wrathful man stirreth up strife; but he that is slow to anger appeaseth strife. (Proverbs 15:18)**
>
> **Surely...the forcing of wrath bringeth forth strife. (Proverbs 30:33)**

STRIFE

Strife is quarreling, fighting, or conflict. It means a clash or dispute. In addition to wrath causing strife, hatred also causes it:

> **Hatred stirreth up strifes; but love covereth all sins. (Proverbs 10:12)**

Forward [aggressive] men also cause strife:

A forward man soweth strife... (Proverbs 16:28)

Pride causes strife:

He that is of a proud heart stirreth up strife... (Proverbs 28:25)

Angry men cause strife:

An angry man stirreth up strife, and a furious man aboundeth in transgression. (Proverbs 29:22)

Scornful men cause strife:

Cast out the scorner, and contention shall go out; yea strife and reproach shall cease. (Proverbs 22:10)

To be scornful is to mock or show contempt for something or someone.

People who meddle, are argumentative, and talk about others cause strife:

He that passeth by, and meddleth with strife belonging not to him, is like one that taketh a dog by the ears...

Where no wood is, there the fire goeth out: so where there is no talebearer, the strife ceaseth.

As coals are to burning coals and wood to fire; so is a contentious man to kindle strife. (Proverbs 26:17,20-21)

Foolish questions cause strife:

But foolish and unlearned questions avoid, knowing that they do gender strifes. (II Timothy 2:23)

Strife is a carnal work of the flesh:

For ye are yet carnal: for whereas there is among you envying, and strife, and divisions, are ye not carnal, and walk as men? (I Corinthians 3:3)

Where envy and strife is, there will be confusion:

But if ye have bitter envying and strife in your hearts, glory not...For where envying and strife is, there is confusion and every evil work. (James 3:14,16)

The Bible says nothing should be done through strife:

> **Let nothing be done through strife or vainglory; but in lowliness of mind let each esteem others better than themselves. (Philippians 2:3)**

Strife is one of the characteristics of false teachers:

> **He is proud, knowing nothing, but doting about questions and strifes of words, whereof cometh envy, strife, railings, evil surmisings.**
>
> **Perverse disputings of men of corrupt minds, and destitute of the truth... (I Timothy 6:4-5)**

SEDITIONS

Sedition is the stirring up of unrest or discord. This passage on the works of the flesh is one of the few where this term is used in the Bible.

HERESIES

Heresies are beliefs contrary to the Word of God. They are opinions of man which are in error and lead to division in the church. Heresies are characteristic of false prophets:

> **But there were false prophets also among the people, even as there shall be false teachers among you, who privily shall bring in damnable heresies... (II Peter 2:1)**

ENVYINGS

Envy is jealousy excited by the success of others. It is resentment of the spiritual, financial, or material blessings of others. It is wrong longing and desire.

Envy is one of the characteristics of false teachers:

> **He is proud knowing nothing, but doting about questions and strifes of words, whereof cometh envy, strife, railings, evil surmisings. (I Timothy 6:4)**

Envy comes from the spirit of man:

> **Do ye think that the Scripture saith in vain, The spirit that dwelleth in us lusteth to envy? (James 4:4)**

Envy is a sign of being a carnal Christian:

For ye are yet carnal: for whereas there is among you envying, and strife, and divisions, are ye not carnal, and walk as men? (I Corinthians 3:3)

Those living in sin are filled with envy:

Being filled with all unrighteousness, fornication, wickedness, covetousness, maliciousness; full of envy, murder, debate, deceit, malignity, whisperers... (Romans 1:29)

For we ourselves also were sometimes foolish, disobedient, and deceived, serving divers lusts and pleasures, living in malice and envy, hateful, and hating one another. (Titus 3:3)

Where there is envy, other problems arise:

But if ye have bitter envying and strife in your hearts, glory not, and lie not against the truth...For where envying and strife is, there is confusion and every evil work. (James 3:14,16)

We are warned not to envy sinners:

Let not thine heart envy sinners; but be thou in the fear of the Lord all the day long. (Proverbs 23:17)

MURDERERS

To murder is to take the life of another with willful malice and forethought. Murder is not the same as self-defense or an accidental killing. Murder is not the same as imposing the death penalty on a person who has killed someone. This was a judgment established by God in Numbers 35. One of the first commandments given by God was "Thou shalt not kill."

Jesus said:

...thou shalt do no murder... (Matthew 19:18)

You should not be guilty of murder:

But let none of you suffer as a murderer, or as a thief, or as an evildoer, or as a busybody in other men's matters. (I Peter 4:15)

The New Testament expands the meaning of murder to include hatred. If you hate other believers it is like being a murderer:

Whosoever hateth his brother is a murderer; and ye know that no murderer hath eternal life abiding in him. (I John 3:15)

DRUNKENNESS

Drunkenness is a condition of having mental and physical faculties affected by excessive drinking. It is intoxication caused by strong chemical drinks. The Bible warns that the drunkard will be poor:

For the drunkard and the glutton shall come to poverty... (Proverbs 23:21)

You are not to live a drunken lifestyle:

Let us walk honestly, as in the day; not in rioting and drunkenness, not in chambering and wantonness, not in strife and envying. (Romans 13:13)

You are not even to keep company with those who are drunkards:

But now I have written unto you not to keep company, if any man that is called a brother be a fornicator, or covetous, or an idolater, or a railer, or a drunkard, or an extortioner; with such an one go not to eat. (I Corinthians 5:11)

The Bible warns that drunkards will not inherit the Kingdom of God:

Know ye not that the unrighteous shall not inherit the kingdom of God? Be not deceived; neither...drunkards...shall inherit the kingdom of God. (I Corinthians 6:9-10)

You may have been a drunkard in times past, but as a believer you are no longer to do this:

That he no longer should live the rest of his time in the flesh to the lusts of men, but to the will of God.

For the time past of our life may suffice us to have wrought the will of the Gentiles, when walked in lasciviousness, lusts, excess of wine, revellings, banquetings, and abominable idolatries...(I Peter 4:2-3)

The Bible contrasts being drunk with wine and being filled with the Spirit:

And be not drunk with wine, wherein is excess; but be filled with the Spirit. (Ephesians 5:18)

In the natural world, a drunkard...

1. Is consumed with desire for drink.
2. Yields control of his emotional, and physical faculties to drink.
3. Has his speech affected by the drink.
4. Is free from inhibitions. He has no fear and often has great strength.
5. Is joyful while under the influence of intoxicants.

REVELLINGS

Revelling is to engage and delight in worldly pleasures, participating in worldly, boisterous merry making or festivity. It is riotous and wild living.

You may have been a reveller in times past, but as a believer you are no longer to behave this way:

> **That he no longer should live the rest of his time in the flesh to the lusts of men, but to the will of God.**
>
> **For the time past of our life may suffice us to have wrought the will the Gentiles, when we walked in lasciviousness...(I Peter 4:2-3)**

WORKS OF THE FLESH: THE RESULT

Paul explains the results of doing the works of the flesh:

> **...of the which I tell you before, as I have also told you in time past, that they which do such things shall not inherit the kingdom of God. (Galatians 5:21)**

God has given a way to avoid this penalty:

> **If we confess our sins, He is faithful and just to forgive us our sins and to cleanse us from all unrighteousness. (I John 1:9)**

WALK IN THE SPIRIT

How does one stop doing the sinful works of the flesh?

First: Repent of your sin and have faith towards God through accepting Jesus Christ as personal Savior:

> **Therefore if any man be in Christ, he is a new creature: old things are passed away; behold, all things are become new. (II Corinthians 5:17)**

God does not take sinful man and give him a self-improvement course. He creates a new creature. The old things pass away. The works of the flesh are to be replaced by the fruit of the Holy Spirit.

Second: Be filled with the Holy Spirit. It is the Holy Spirit who will enable you to walk in the ways of the Spirit instead of the sinful ways of the flesh:

> **This I say then, Walk in the Spirit, and ye shall not fulfill the lust of the flesh. (Galatians 5:17)**

Third: Realize you cannot be freed from the works of the flesh and walk in the Spirit through your own effort.

The Apostle Paul described the struggle he had in his own effort to live a Godly life:

> **For that which I do I allow not: for what I would, that do I not; but what I hate, that do I.**
>
> **If then I do that which I would not, I consent unto the law that it is good.**
>
> **Now then it is no more I that do it, but sin that dwelleth in me.**
>
> **For I know that in me (that is, in my flesh) dwelleth no good thing: for to will is present with me; but how to perform that which is good I find not.**
>
> **For the good that I would I do not: but the evil which I would not, that I do. (Romans 7:15-19)**

Paul experienced the difficulty of living a holy life but he continued to pursue this goal despite his failures.

Ask God to put a desire to be holy in your heart. Whenever you fail and sin, confess it immediately and ask the Holy Spirit to help you overcome it. This is how you learn to walk in the Spirit and...

> **There is therefore now no condemnation to them which are in Christ Jesus, who walk not after the flesh but after the Spirit.**
>
> **For the law of the Spirit of life in Christ Jesus hath made me free from the law of sin and death...**

That the righteousness of the law might be fulfilled in us who walk not after the flesh, but after the Spirit.

For they that are after the flesh do mind the things of the flesh; but they that are after the Spirit the things of the Spirit.

For to be carnally minded is death; but to be spiritually minded is life and peace.

Because the carnal mind is enmity against God; for it is not subject to the law of God, neither indeed can be.

So then they that are in the flesh cannot please God.

But ye are not in the flesh, but in the Spirit, if so be that the Spirit of God dwell in you. (Romans 8:1-9)

The fruit of Christ-like qualities only develop as you walk in the power of the Holy Spirit. This is why it is so important for believers to understand the ministry of the Holy Spirit.

SELF-TEST

1. Write the Key Verses from memory.

____

____

____

____

2. The qualities contrasting the fruit of the Holy Spirit are called:

____

____

____

3. What Bible passage gives the key to overcoming the works of the flesh?

____

____

____

4. On the following page, look at the works of the flesh in list one. Read the definitions in list two. Write the number which describes the work of the flesh on the blank provided.

List One	**List Two**
_____Revellings	1. Sex by a married person with someone other than their spouse.
_____Envyings	2. Sexual intercourse by two people not married to each other.
_____Murders	3. Spiritually and morally sinful.
_____Drunkenness	4. Lust, sinful emotions, lewdness.
_____Lasciviousness	5. Worship of idols.
_____Adultery	6. Practice of witches.
_____Fornication	7. Opposite of love.
_____Uncleanness	8. Disagreement, dissension.
_____Witchcraft	9. Rivalry, desire to copy others to equal or excel them.
_____Idolatry	10. Violent anger, rage.
_____Hatred	11. Quarreling, fighting.
_____Variance	12. Stirring up discord.
_____Heresies	13. Beliefs contrary to God's Word.
_____Emulations	14. Jealousy excited by the success of others.
_____Strife	15. Taking the life of another.
Wrath	16. Excessive drinking.
_____Seditions	17. Worldly, boisterous merry-making or festivities.

(Answers to tests are provided at the conclusion of the final chapter in this manual.)

FOR FURTHER STUDY

Contrast the fruit of the Spirit in Galatians 5:22-24 with the works of the flesh listed in Galatians 5:19-21. The first one is done as an example for you to follow:

CONTRASTS

Fruit Of The Spirit (Galatians 5:22-24)	**Works Of The Flesh (Galatians 5:19-21)**
Love	Hatred, murder, envy
Joy	
Peace	
Longsuffering	
Gentleness	
Goodness	
Faith	
Meekness	
Temperance	

CHAPTER THIRTEEN

DEVELOPING SPIRITUAL FRUIT

OBJECTIVES:

Upon completion of this chapter you will be able to:

- Explain the different production levels of spiritual fruit.
- Use the parallel of natural fruit production to explain how the fruit of the Spirit is developed in the life of a believer.

KEY VERSE:

> **Every branch in me that beareth not fruit, He taketh away; and every branch that beareth fruit, He purgeth it, that it may bring for more fruit. (John 15:2)**

INTRODUCTION

The key verse for this chapter confirms it is God's desire that spiritual fruit be evident in your life. This chapter provides guidelines for developing spiritual fruit.

PRODUCTION LEVELS OF FRUIT

There are different levels of fruit bearing evident in the lives of believers. John chapter 15 identifies the various levels of fruit production:

-Fruit:	John 15:2a
-More fruit:	John 15:2b
-Much fruit:	John 15:5,8
-Permanent Fruit:	John 15:16

God's desire is that you bear much spiritual fruit and that it is permanent. He wants you to be productive in the outer fruit of evangelism and the inner fruit of Christ-likeness.

NATURAL AND SPIRITUAL TRUTHS

The Bible contains important principles which you must identify in order to understand what God is saying to you through His Word. One of these principles is that of natural parallels of spiritual truths. The word "parallel" means to be similar to something or to "lay side by side." In a "natural parallel of a spiritual truth" God uses a natural example to explain or represent a spiritual truth.

The parables of Jesus were natural examples of spiritual truths. For example, in one parable He used the natural example of a woman searching intensely for a lost coin. He used this to illustrate the intense concern we should have for men and women who are lost in sin. This is just one of many examples of parables in which Jesus used natural examples to illustrate spiritual truths.

This principle of natural and spiritual parallels is explained in I Corinthians:

> **...There is a natural body, and there is a spiritual body.**
>
> **And so it is written, The first man Adam was made a living soul; the last Adam was made a quickening spirit.**
>
> **Howbeit that was not first which was spiritual but that which is natural; and afterward that which is spiritual. (I Corinthians 15:44-46)**

In these verses the Apostle Paul shared one of the greatest examples of a natural parallel of a spiritual truth. The first man created by God was the natural man, Adam. Jesus, who is called the last Adam, was a spirit. Adam was a natural parallel of the spiritual truth God revealed through Jesus Christ. By the natural man came sin and death. By the spiritual man came salvation and life.

That which is natural is something you can observe with your senses; you can see, hear or touch it. That which is spiritual can only be observed with spiritual senses. Natural examples can be recognized with the physical senses. Their spiritual parallels can only be recognized through the revelation of the Holy Spirit. Understanding this principle of natural parallels of spiritual truths results in new insights in the study of God's Word.

DEVELOPING THE FRUIT OF THE SPIRIT

Jesus used the term "fruit" of the Spirit as a natural parallel of a spiritual truth. Certain conditions are necessary to produce fruit in the natural world. These are spiritual parallels of things necessary for production of spiritual fruit. In the natural world, as well as the spiritual realm, there are specific conditions necessary to assure growth. These include the following:

LIFE:

The first requirement for development of the fruit of the Spirit is life. Just as life in the natural world comes through seed, life in the spiritual world came through the Seed of Jesus Christ.

In the first promise of a Savior of the world, Jesus was called a Seed:

> **And I will put enmity between thee and the woman, and between thy seed and her seed; it shall bruise thy head, and thou shalt bruise his heel. (Genesis 3:15)**
>
> **In Jesus Christ [the Seed] is the life required to produce spiritual fruit:**
>
> **In Him was life; and the life was the light of men. (John 1:4)**
>
> **For as the Father hath life in Himself; so hath He given to the Son to have life in Himself. (John 5:26)**
>
> **...I am come that they might have life and that they might have it more abundantly. (John 10:10)**

That Seed of life, Jesus Christ, must be living in you. You cannot produce the fruit of the Spirit if you do not have a personal relationship with Him because...

> **From Me is thy fruit found... (Hosea 14:8)**

WATER:

Water is necessary to produce fruit in the natural world. Water is one of the symbols of the Holy Spirit. The water of the Holy Spirit is necessary to produce fruit in the spirit world. It quenches your spiritual thirst and brings spiritual growth:

> **He that believeth on Me, as the Scripture hath said, out of his belly shall flow rivers of living water.**
>
> **(But this spake He of the Spirit, which they that believe on Him should receive; for the Holy Ghost was not yet given, because that Jesus was not yet glorified.) (John 7:38-39)**
>
> **For I will pour water upon him that is thirsty, and floods upon the dry ground: I will pour my spirit upon thy seed, and my blessing upon thine offspring. (Isaiah 44:3)**

LIGHT:

It is response to light that stimulates growth in the natural fruit bearing process. It is your response to the light of God's Word that produces the fruit of the Spirit.

> **This is the message which we have heard of Him, and declare unto you, that God is light, and in Him is no darkness at all.**
>
> **If we say that we have fellowship with Him and walk in darkness, we lie, and do not the truth;**
>
> **But if we walk in the light as He is in the light, we have fellowship one with another, and the blood of Jesus Christ His son cleanseth us from all sin. (I John 1:5-7)**

AIR:

Carbon dioxide is drawn in by the natural plant from the air which surrounds it. This is necessary for growth and fruit production. In the Word of God the Holy Spirit is compared to air or wind:

> **The wind breathes where it will, and thou canst hear the sound of it; but knowest thou nothing of the way it came or the way it goes; so it is when a man is born on the breath of the spirit. (John 3:8, Knox Translation)**

The "wind" of the Holy Spirit blowing across your life is much like the wind in the natural world. It scatters the seeds of the Word of God, separates the wheat from the chaff in your spiritual life, and fans the dying coals of your spiritual zeal to set you ablaze for God.

SPACE:

In Matthew 13 in the parable of the sower, competition for space choked out some plants. The believer who develops spiritual fruit will discover he must be set apart from the competition of the world:

> **He also that received seed among the thorns is he that heareth the word; and the care of this world, and the deceitfulness of riches, choke the word, and he becometh unfruitful. (Matthew 13:22)**

You are not to be conformed to the ways of the world. You are to be transformed [changed] into the ways of God:

And be not conformed to this world; but be ye transformed by the renewing of your mind... (Romans 12:2a)

God clears space around you [sets you apart from the world] to permit you to grow spiritually:

...He shall grow as the lily, and cast forth his roots as Lebanon. His branches shall spread, and his beauty shall be as the olive tree and his smell as Lebanon.

They that dwell under his shadow shall return; they shall revive as the corn and grow as the vine...From Me is thy fruit found. (Hosea 14:5-8)

ROOT SYSTEM:

Roots are necessary to anchor and supply nutrients to the plant. Psalms chapter 1 tells how to develop the root system in your spiritual life:

Blessed is the man that walketh not in the counsel of the ungodly, nor standeth in the way of sinners, nor sitteth in the seat of the scornful.

But his delight is in the law of the Lord; and in His law doth he meditate day and night.

And he shall be like a tree planted by the rivers of water, that bringeth forth his fruit in his season; his leaf also shall not wither; and whatsoever he doeth shall prosper. (Psalms 1:1-3)

REST:

Dormancy [rest] occupies a specific season in the natural growth cycle of plants. Dormancy is a period during which the plant may appear to be dead because there is no growth. It is a period of rest for the plant. Dormancy usually occurs right before a period of very rapid growth. In the natural world, God commanded times of rest for the land (Leviticus 25:5).

One of the purposes of the baptism of the Holy Spirit is to bring spiritual rest and refreshing. This spiritual refreshing results in rapid growth of the fruit of the Holy Spirit:

Let us fear, lest a promise being left us of entering into his rest, any of you would seem to come short of it.

There remaineth therefore a rest to the people of God. (Hebrews 4:1,9)
For with stammering lips and another tongue will He speak to this people.

To whom He said, This is the rest wherewith ye may cause the weary to rest; and this is the refreshing... (Isaiah 28:11-12)

SOIL:

Both in the natural and spiritual worlds, in order to produce fruit the ground must be properly prepared. In the parable of the sower in Matthew 13 it was the condition of the soil that affected the growth of the seed. Your heart is like soil in the natural world. If your heart is hard and filled with things of the world that choke out the Word of God, you will not bear spiritual fruit.

It is your responsibility to prepare the spiritual soil of your heart to respond properly to God's Word:

Sow to yourselves in righteousness, reap in mercy; break up your fallow ground: for it is time to seek the Lord, till He come and rain righteousness upon you. (Hosea 10:12)

DEATH:

Every time you plant a seed to produce fruit, it does not come to life unless it dies first:

Verily, verily, I say unto you, Except a corn of wheat fall into the ground and die, it abideth alone: but if it die, it bringeth forth much fruit. (John 12:24)

Everytime you plant a seed, you sow something that does not come to life [germinating, springing up, and growing] unless it dies first. (I Corinthians 15:36, The Amplified Bible)

Spiritual life depends on death to the things of the world. It requires death to sin, worldly desires, and pleasures. Death to the world results in the development of the fruit of Christ-likeness in your life.

ATTACHED TO THE VINE:

In order to bear fruit in the natural world a branch must be attached to the main plant. If the branch is broken off from the main life-giving vine it will not bear fruit. Jesus is the vine and we are the branches. In order to bear spiritual fruit we must maintain our relationship to Him:

I am the true vine, and My Father is the husbandman.

Every branch in me that beareth not fruit He taketh away; and every branch that beareth fruit, He purgeth it, that it may bring forth more fruit...

Abide in Me, and I in you. As the branch cannot bear fruit of itself, except it abide in the vine; no more can ye, except ye abide in Me.

I am the vine, ye are the branches: He that abideth in Me, and I in him, the same bringeth forth much fruit: for without Me ye can do nothing. (John 15:1-5)

PRUNING:

Pruning is necessary in the natural world if a plant is to remain reproductive and bear fruit. When a farmer prunes a plant he cuts off the unproductive branches in order to make the plant produce more fruit. He removes everything which would hinder the growth of the plant.

Pruning is also necessary in the spiritual world. Spiritual pruning is correction by God. The Bible also calls it chastisement. When God "prunes" He removes from your life everything which would hinder your spiritual growth. This process is necessary if you are to bear spiritual fruit:

Every branch in Me that beareth not fruit, He taketh away; and every branch that beareth fruit, He purgeth it, that it may bring forth more fruit. (John 15:2)

Sometimes you do not reap the benefits of pruning because you blame Satan when God is actually the one bringing circumstances into your life to correct [prune] you. The purpose of God's correction is given in Hosea:

Come, and let us return unto the Lord; for He hath torn, and He will heal us; He hath smitten and He will bind us up. (Hosea 6:1)

The chastisement of pruning results in returning to God. Only by returning to Him will you become spiritually reproductive and bear the fruit of the Holy Spirit.

CLIMATE:

Climate is important in development of fruit. In the natural world, many types of fruit are developed in environments that are specially controlled. They are grown in buildings called "hot houses" at specific temperatures. They are protected from the real environment of the outside world. If you take a "hot house" plant and move it outside, it will soon die because it has lived only in a controlled environment. It cannot withstand the environment of the real world.

Spiritually speaking, we do not want "hot house" Christians who look good in controlled settings but wilt on contact with the real world. Spiritual fruit should be just as evident in our contacts with the world as it is in the controlled settings of Christian friends or the church.

SELF-TEST

1. Write the Key Verse from memory.

____

____

____

2. What are four production levels of fruit mentioned in John chapter 15?

____

____

____

____

3. List twelve things necessary in the natural world for fruit production. Remember, these are natural parallels of a spiritual truth because these are also necessary for the production of spiritual fruit.

_______________	_______________
_______________	_______________
_______________	_______________
_______________	_______________
_______________	_______________
_______________	_______________

(Answers to tests are provided at the conclusion of the final chapter in this manual.)

FOR FURTHER STUDY

1. Read Song Of Solomon 4:12-16. In this passage we are given a glimpse of God's garden. He calls His people, the Church [believers] His garden. Your life is spiritual "ground" that will either yield spiritual fruit, spiritual "weeds", or be barren and empty. What is growing in the spiritual ground of your life? Are there weeds and thorns of:

   -The cares, anxieties, worries or interests of this world?
   -The deceitfulness of riches?
   -The desire for worldly things?

   What takes up the most space in your life? What occupies most of your time and attention? What is most important in your priorities? Is the "garden of your heart" stony soil? Do you have a hard heart? Those areas in which you stubbornly refuse to comply with Christ's commands are barren, rocky spiritual soil.

2. This lesson completes your study of the *"Ministry Of the Holy Spirit."* For further study we suggest you obtain the Harvestime International Institute course entitled "Spiritual Strategies: A Manual Of Spiritual Warfare." It concerns the function of the Holy Spirit in spiritual warfare and explains the ministries of the other members of the Trinity, God the Father and Jesus Christ the Son.

3. Complete the "Spiritual Fruit Analysis" which follows. Your honest answers will help you evaluate the present level of development of spiritual fruit in your life.

SPIRITUAL FRUIT ANALYSIS

Read each of the statements and respond by selecting the number of the response which best describes you at present. Respond to each questions by writing either 3, 2, 1, or 0.

3 means "this is definitely true in my life."
2 means "this is usually true in my life."
1 means "this is occasionally true."
0 means "this is never true in my life."

Example: __2__1. I am secure in the certainty of God's control of the future.

(The person taking this analysis wrote the number "2" in the blank because this statement is usually true in their life).

______1. I am secure in the certainty of God's control of the future.
______2. I am aware that Jesus willingly did God's will.
______3. I am agreeing that my faith has power only if God is trustworthy.
______4. I am waiting for God's promises to be fulfilled.
______5. I think of God as sometimes angry.
______6. I know that God's mercy, revealed by sending Jesus, spared me from deserved punishment.
______7. I am grateful that God so loved the world that He gave His Son, Jesus Christ.
______8. I know that God's presence is my joy.
______9. I am saying "no" to what God forbids and "yes" to His commands.
______10. I am accepting Jesus' promise of peace.
______11. I am willingly yielding to authorities in my life.
______12. I am believing Jesus Christ is the same yesterday, today, and forever.
______13. I accept the imperfections of others, knowing God is still at work in their lives.
______14. I am under conviction by a stern but good God.
______15. I am forgiving others as Christ forgave me.
______16. I know God loves me even when I am not loving to others.
______17. I have assurance of salvation from receiving Jesus as Lord.
______18. I am learning to say "no" to lesser things in order to experience greater things for God.
______19. I have an assurance of forgiveness of sins.
______20. I am in willing submission to God's Word and the Holy Spirit.
______21. I am being reliable in fulfilling promises.
______22. I have perseverance in the face of frustration, persecution, difficult demands, and pressures.
______23. I am conducting my everyday activities in a Biblical lifestyle.
______24. I am comforting, encouraging, and counseling others.
______25. I am meeting the needs of relatives and friends unconditionally.
______26. I am growing and maturing as God intends.
______27. I am having a consistent devotional life.
______28. I have inner assurance and confidence from being right with God [righteousness].
______29. I am expressing cooperation, teachability, and humility.
______30. I am being dependable in an accepted responsibility.
______31. I am waiting for God to assist me in becoming what I can be as intended by Him.
______32. I am faithful in telling the truth, honesty, and keeping promises.
______33. I am speaking positive words which build up others.
______34. I am affirming the good qualities of people who "get on my nerves."
______35. I have consistent satisfaction from doing God's will.

_____36. I am relating to a person or group to keep me accountable in controlling problem areas in my life.

_____37. I am at peace within by allowing the Holy Spirit to control my inner life.

_____38. I am open to suggestions from others as to where I need to improve.

_____39. I am doing well with my abilities of which I am aware.

_____40. I have postponed activities which provide immediate pleasure for purposes of future spiritual growth.

_____41. I have confronted other Christians in a caring way when their conduct is wrong by God's standards.

_____42. I am listening in order to really understand another person.

_____43. I am serving others who cannot or will not serve me.

_____44. I have great delight in a spiritual achievement.

_____45. I am acting constructively on my knowledge of control problems in my life such as money, sex, overeating, or gossip.

_____46. I have calmness within when experiencing conflict of differences with others.

_____47. I am meek in my conversation.

_____48. I am managing my time, money, and self as they are owned by God.

_____49. I am continuing to hope in God, even when I am suffering.

_____50. I am letting "my light so shine before men that they may see my good works..."

_____51. I see a need with compassion and respond to it helpfully.

_____52. I have forgiven others who have deeply hurt me.

_____53. I find joy in what God is doing in the lives of other believers.

_____54. I have an untroubled heart in the midst of this world's distress.

_____55. I am avoiding "getting even" when others do me wrong.

_____56. I can be counted on in times of distress.

_____57. I am accepting others who develop at a different pace or in a different direction.

_____58. I sign petitions against unjust practices.

_____59. I am accepting of another person considered by others to be practicing a "serious" sin.

_____60. I am praying for my enemies and those who are unloving.

_____61. I am rejoicing in completing my commitments of ministry.

_____62. I am avoiding situations where I am easily tempted or addicted.

SCORING THE ANALYSIS

1. Transfer your answers from the "Analysis" to the blanks on the next page.. For example, if you answered Question 1 with a "3", then write "3" in the number 1 square.

2. After you have filled in every square, compute the totals by adding across the row.

➪	➪	➪	➪	➪	➪	➪	Row Total	FRUIT
1	10	19	28	37	46	55		Peace
2	11	20	29	38	47	56		Gentleness
3	12	21	30	39	48	57		Faith
4	13	22	31	40	49	58		Long Suffering
5	14	23	32	41	50	59		Goodness
6	15	24	33	42	51	60		Meekness
7	16	25	34	43	52	61		Love
8	17	26	35	44	53	62		Joy
9	18	27	36	45	54	63		Temperance

APPLICATION

On the basis of the results of your Spiritual Fruit Analysis, complete the following statements:

1. Look at your lowest scores, then complete the following statement:

   The analysis suggests that I need further development of the spiritual fruit of:

____

2. I am choosing one fruit to focus my prayers and attention on during the next month. The fruit I will focus on is__________________.

3. In addition to prayer, I will take the following actions to aid the development of this fruit: Check one and then complete the statement:

   ____I will start doing something new.

   What will you start doing?____

   ____I will stop doing something I am now doing.

   What will you stop doing?____

   ____I will change something in my life.

   What specifically will you change?____________________________________

APPENDIX

The Amplified Bible translation of passages on spiritual gifts provides additional insight into the meaning of the various gifts:

-And His gifts were varied; He Himself appointed and gave men to us some to be apostles (special messengers), some prophets (inspired preachers and expounders), some evangelists (preachers of the Gospel, traveling missionaries); some pastors (shepherds of His flock) and teachers.

His intention was the perfecting and the full equipping of the saints (His consecrated people) that they should do the work of ministering toward building up Christ's body (the church),

That it might develop until we all attain oneness in the faith and in the comprehension (the full and accurate knowledge) of the Son of God; that we might arrive at really mature manhood (the completeness of personality) which is nothing less than the standard height of Christ's own perfection (the measure of the stature of the fullness of the Christ, and the completeness found in Him).

So then we may no longer be children, tossed like ships to and fro between chance gusts of teaching, and wavering with every changing wind of doctrine, (the prey of) the cunning and cleverness of unscrupulous men engaged in every form of trickery in inventing errors to mislead.

Rather, let our lives lovingly express truth in all things - speaking truly, dealing truly, living truly enfolded in love, let us grow up in every way and in all things unto Him, Who is the Head even Christ, the Messiah, the Anointed One. (Ephesians 4:11-17)

-Practice hospitality to one another - that is, those of the household of faith. Be hospitable, that is, be a lover of strangers, with brotherly affection for the unknown guests, the foreigners, the poor and all others who come your way who are of Christ's body. And in each instance do it ungrudgingly - cordially and graciously without complaining but as representing Him.

As each of you has received a gift (a particular spiritual talent, a gracious divine endowment) employ it for one another as benefits good trustees of God's many-sided grace - faithful stewards of the extremely divers powers and gifts granted to Christians by unmerited favor.

Whoever speaks let him do it as one who utters oracles of God; whoever renders service let him do it with the strength which God furnishes abundantly; so that in all things God may be glorified through Jesus Christ the Messiah... (I Peter 4:9-11)

-For as in one physical body we have many parts (organs, members) and all of these parts do not have the same function or use,

So we, numerous as we are, are one body in Christ, the Messiah, and individually we are parts one of another- mutually dependent on one another.

Having gifts (faculties, talents, qualities) that differ according to the grace given us, let us use them: He whose gift is prophecy, let him prophesy according to the proportion of his faith.

He whose gift is practical service, let him give himself to serving; he who teaches, to his teaching;

He who exhorts, (encourages) to his exhortation; he who contributes, let him do it in simplicity and liberality; he who gives aid and superintends, with zeal and singleness of mind; he who does acts of mercy, with genuine cheerfulness and joyful eagerness. (Romans 12:4-8)

-Now about the spiritual gifts (the special endowments of supernatural energy) brethren, I do not want you to be misinformed...

Now there are distinctive varieties and distributions of endowments (extraordinary powers distinguishing certain Christians due to the power of divine grace or action in their souls by the Holy Spirit) and they vary, but the Holy Spirit remains the same.

And there are distinctive varieties of service and ministration, but it is the same Lord who is served.

And there are distinctive varieties of operation - of working to accomplish things - but is it is the same God who inspires and energizes them all in all.

But to each one is given the manifestation of the Holy Spirit - that is the evidence, the spiritual illumination of the Spirit - for good and profit.

To one is given in and through the Holy Spirit the power to speak a message of wisdom, and to another the power to express a word of knowledge and understanding according to the same Holy Spirit;

To another wonder-working faith by the same Holy Spirit, to another the extraordinary powers of healing by the one Spirit;

To another the working of miracles, to another prophetic insight - that is, the gift of interpreting the divine will and purpose; to another the ability to discern and distinguish between the utterances of true spirits and false ones, to another various kinds of unknown tongues, to another the ability to interpret such tongues.

All these achievements and abilities are inspired and brought to pass by one and the same Holy Spirit who apportions to each person individually exactly as He chooses....

Now you (collectively) are Christ's body and (individually) you are members of it, each part severally and distinct - each with his own place and function.

So God has appointed some in the church for His own use: First apostles (special messengers); second apostles (inspired preachers and expounders); third teachers, then wonder-workers, then those with ability to heal the sick, helpers, administrators, speakers in different (unknown) tongues. (I Corinthians 12, selected verses)

ANSWERS TO SELF-TESTS

CHAPTER ONE:

1. And Jesus, when He was baptized, went up straightway out of the water; and, lo, the heavens were opened unto Him, and He saw the Spirit of God descending like a dove, and lighting upon Him; And lo a voice from heaven saying, This is my beloved Son, in whom I am well pleased. (Matthew 3:16-17)

2. Father, Son, Holy Spirit.

3. The Holy Spirit:
   -Has a mind.
   -Searches out the human mind.
   -Has a will.
   -Speaks.
   -Loves.
   -Intercedes.

4. This means He has feelings that can be affected by the actions of man.

5. -Lie to the Spirit.
   -Resist the Spirit.
   -Quench the Spirit.
   -Grieve the Spirit.
   -Insult the Spirit.
   -Blaspheme the Spirit.
   -Vex the Spirit.

6. 5,3,2,1,4

CHAPTER TWO:

1. Know ye not that ye are the temple of God, and that the Spirit of God dwelleth in you? (I Corinthians 3:16)

2. An emblem represents something. It is a symbol which has a special meaning.

3. 5,4,3,1,2

4. -The presence of the Lord
   -Approval

-Protection/Guidance
-Purifying
-The gift of the Holy Spirit
-Judgment

5. -The Spirit of God
-The Spirit of Christ
-Eternal Spirit
-Spirit of Truth
-Spirit of Grace
-Spirit of Life
-Spirit of Glory
-Spirit of Wisdom and Revelation
-The Comforter
-Spirit of Promise
-Spirit of Holiness
-Spirit of Faith
-Spirit of Adoption

CHAPTER THREE:

1. But the Comforter, which is the Holy Ghost, whom the Father will send in my name, He shall teach you all things, and bring all things to your remembrance, whatsoever I have said unto you. (John 14:26)

2. -He came upon the leaders of Israel.
-He came upon their places of worship.
-He guided them to the Promised Land.
-He will come upon Israel during the Tribulation.
-He will come upon Israel during the Millennium.

3. True.

4. 2, 1, 3

5. John 16:7-11

6. The Holy Spirit is the restraining spiritual force that limits the power of Satan.

7. Jesus was:
-Conceived by the Spirit.
-Anointed by the Spirit.
-Sealed by the Spirit.

-Led by the Spirit.
-Empowered by the Spirit.
-Filled by the Spirit.
-Troubled in the Spirit.
-Rejoiced in the Spirit.
-Offered through the Spirit.
-Raised from the dead by the Spirit.
-Commanded His disciples through the Spirit.

8. The Holy Spirit:
-Formed it.
-Inspires its worship.
-Directs its missionary activities.
-Selects its ministers.
-Anoints its preachers.
-Guides its decisions.
-Baptizes it with power.

9. The Holy Spirit:
-Convicts
-Sanctifies
-Dwells within
-Unites
-Guides
-Conforms to the image of Christ
-Gives assurance of salvation
-Gives liberty
-Empowers for witnessing
-Demonstrates God`s power
-Regenerates
-Baptizes
-Strengthens
-Intercedes
-Demonstrates love
-Reveals truth
-Teaches
-Speaks through him
-Comforts
-Quickens

10. They become a powerful witness of the Gospel. Acts 1:8.

CHAPTER FOUR:

1. But ye shall receive power after that the Holy Ghost is come upon you: and ye shall be witnesses unto me both in Jerusalem, and in all Judaea, and in Samaria, and unto the uttermost part of the earth. (Acts 1:8)

2. -Repent and be baptized
-Believe it is for you
-Desire it
-Accept it as a gift
-Yield to God

-Request the prayers of other believers

3. Speaking in a language not known to the speaker.

4. To make the Christian a powerful witness for the Gospel. Acts 1:8.

5. -Every Christian receives the Holy Spirit when he is converted.
-The Bible says not all speak with tongues.
-Fear.
-It is an emotional experience.

6. No.

7. To completely immerse or submerge in something.

8. -Acts 2:2-4
-Acts 10:44-46
-Acts 19:6

CHAPTER FIVE:

1. Now concerning spiritual gifts, brethren, I would not have you ignorant. (I Corinthians 12:1)

2. A talent is a natural ability inherited at birth or developed through training. A spiritual gift is a supernatural ability which did not come by inheritance or training. It is a supernatural ability given by the Holy Spirit for specific spiritual purposes.

3. -Perfect the saints.
-Promote the work of the ministry.
-Edify Christ and the Church.

4. We will:
-Become united in the faith.
-Develop our knowledge of Christ.
-Develop in perfection, with Christ as our model.
-Become stable, not deceived by false doctrines.
-Mature spiritually in Christ.

5. Yes. I Peter 4:10 and I Corinthians 12:7 and 11.

6. -Not using gifts given to you.
-Attempting to use gifts not given to you.

-Not using gifts properly.
-Glorifying your gift.

7. The Holy Spirit.

8. Love. I Corinthians 13.

9. Counterfeit gifts do not fulfill the Scriptural purposes for spiritual gifts given in Ephesians 4:12-15. They do not agree with what the Bible teaches about Jesus. Those who are counterfeit will display personal characteristics such as listed in II Peter 2 and Jude.

10. Spiritual gifts are supernatural abilities given by the Holy Spirit to believers to enable effective ministry.

11. All spiritual gifts are for today because the purposes for which they were given are not yet fulfilled. Spiritual gifts will operate until "that which is perfect" comes. This means the establishing of Christ's kingdom on earth.

12. The gift of the Holy Spirit was given on the day of Pentecost. Gifts of the Holy Spirit are supernatural spiritual abilities available for believers.

13. a. T
b. F
c. F
d. F
e. F
f. T
g. T
h. T
i. T

CHAPTER SIX:

1. And He gave some apostles; and some, prophets; and some, evangelists; and some, pastors, and teachers. (Ephesians 4:11)

2. -Apostles
-Prophets
-Evangelists
-Pastors
-Teachers

3. Because each one is a special leadership position in the church.

4. a. True. b. True. c. True.

5. 2,1,4,3,5

6. -Special gifts
-Speaking gifts
-Serving gifts
-Sign gifts

CHAPTER SEVEN:

1. But now hath God set the members every one of them in the body, as it hath pleased Him. (I Corinthians 12:18)

2. -Prophecy
-Teaching
-Exhortation
-Word of wisdom
-Word of knowledge

3. 2,1,4,3,5

4. C

5. False.

CHAPTER EIGHT:

1. And whosoever of you will be the chiefest, shall be servant of all. (Mark 10:44)

2. -Discerning of spirits
-Leadership
-Administration
-Faith
-Giving
-Helps
-Serving
-Mercy
-Hospitality

3. Because they serve to provide structure, organization, and support in both spiritual and practical areas.

4. A person with the gift of administration has the ability to direct, organize, and make decisions on behalf of another. The gift of leadership motivates and leads others to accomplish specific goals for the glory of God.

5. Serving differs from helps in that it relieves someone of certain duties. One who serves assumes the responsibility for certain tasks to free another to exercise their spiritual gift. A person with the gift of helps assists someone in their ministry but does not relieve them of the responsibility.

6. 9,6,2,3,5,7,11,4,8

7. False.

8. The definition of faith is given in Hebrews 11:1.

9. The gift is for power. The fruit is for character.

10. By hearing the Word of God. Romans 10:17.

CHAPTER NINE:

1. How shall we escape, if we neglect so great salvation; which at the first began to be spoken by the Lord, and was confirmed unto us by them that heard Him; God also bearing them witness, both with signs and wonders, and with divers miracles, and gifts of the Holy Ghost, according to His own will? (Hebrews 2:3-4)

2. -Miracles
   -Healing
   -Tongues
   -Interpretation of tongues

3. That ye might believe Jesus is the Christ. That believing you might have life through His name. John 20:30-31.

4. 2,3,4,1

5. a.F; b.T; c.F; d.F; e.T; f.F; g.F; h.F

CHAPTER TEN:

1. Wherefore I put thee in remembrance that thou stir up the gift of God, which is in thee by the putting on of my hands. (Timothy 1:6)

2. -Accomplish purposes and objectives
 -Conduct spiritual warfare
 -Avoid abuse
 -Avoid frustration
 -Assume responsibility

3.

Step One:	Be born again.
Step Two:	Receive the baptism of the Holy Spirit.
Step Three:	Know the spiritual gifts.
Step Four:	Observe models of the gifts.
Step Five:	Seek a spiritual gift.
Step Six:	Laying on of hands.
Step Seven:	Analyze your spiritual interests.
Step Eight:	Analysis by a Christian leader.
Step Nine:	Analyze past Christian service.
Step Ten:	Complete the spiritual gifts questionnaires.
Step Eleven:	Identify gifts you think you might have.
Step Twelve:	Identify spiritual needs.
Step Thirteen:	Fill a spiritual need.
Step Fourteen:	Evaluate your ministry.

CHAPTER ELEVEN:

1. Evangelism; being a powerful witness of the Gospel message.

2. Inner fruit of Christ-like spiritual qualities.

3. Galatians 5:22-23.

-Love	-Joy
-Peace	-Longsuffering
-Gentleness	-Goodness
-Faith	-Meekness

 -Temperance

4. John 15:16

5. But the fruit of the Spirit is love, joy, peace, longsuffering, gentleness, goodness, faith, Meekness, temperance: against such there is no law. (Galatians 5:22-23)

6. 9,7,8,5,6,2,4,1

7. The fruit of the Spirit is important because it is not enough to have the appearance of spirituality. We must have spiritual fruit for it is by this that we are known to be of God. Fruit carries the seeds of reproduction in the spirit world.

8. Peace with God is obtained by being justified and forgiven for sin. Peace of God is received after this experience. It is peace God gives for daily living. (See Romans 5:1 and Philippians 4:7).

CHAPTER TWELVE:

1. Now the works of the flesh are manifest, which are these: Adultery, fornication, uncleanness, lasciviousness,

   Idolatry, witchcraft, hatred, variance, emulations, wrath, strife, seditions, heresies,

   Envyings, murders, drunkenness, revellings, and such like; of the which I tell you before, as I have also told you in time past, that they which do such things shall not inherit the Kingdom of God. (Galatians 5:19-21)

2. Works of the flesh.

3. Galatians 5:16

4. 17,14,15,16,4,1,2,3,6,5,7,8,13,9,11,10,12

CHAPTER THIRTEEN:

1. Every branch in Me that beareth not fruit He taketh away; and every branch that beareth fruit He purgeth it, that it may bring forth more fruit. (John 15:2)

2. Fruit, more fruit, much fruit, permanent fruit.

3. Life, water, light, air, space, root system, rest, soil, death, attached to the vine, pruning, climate.

www.ingramcontent.com/pod-product-compliance
Lightning Source LLC
LaVergne TN
LVHW080319110826
845155LV00026B/162

* 9 7 8 1 9 3 0 7 0 3 0 6 3 *